Venus

Earth

Asteroid Belt

Saturn

 Neptune

Onboard the
Space Shuttle

Onboard the
Space Shuttle

Ray Spangenburg and Kit Moser

Franklin Watts

A DIVISION OF SCHOLASTIC INC.
NEW YORK · TORONTO · LONDON · AUCKLAND
SYDNEY · MEXICO CITY · NEW DELHI · HONG KONG
DANBURY, CONNECTICUT

In memory of
the brave members of
THE *CHALLENGER*, STS-51L, CREW

Photographs © 2002: Corbis-Bettmann: 15, 73; Hulton Archive/Getty Images/Earl Young: 20; NASA: 71, 107 (ESA/STSI), cover, 2, 8, 12, 26, 31, 33, 36, 38, 41, 42, 45, 48, 49, 51, 53, 55, 57, 60, 66, 67, 68, 76, 81, 88, 89, 94, 99, 100, 103, 104, 111; Photo Researchers, NY/David Ducros/SPL: 17.

The photograph on the cover shows astronaut James S. Voss taking pictures while his feet are anchored to the space shuttle *Atlantis*'s remote manipulator system. The photograph opposite the title page shows the launch of the space shuttle *Discovery* on October 29, 1998.

Library of Congress Cataloging-in-Publication Data

    Spangenburg, Ray, 1939-
    Onboard the space shuttle / Ray Spangenburg and Kit Moser.
    p. cm.— (Out of this world)
    Includes bibliographical references and index.
    Summary: Examines what it is like for the crews living and working on American space shuttles and discusses the life of the Russian space station Mir and plans for an international space station.
    ISBN 0-531-11896-7 (lib. bdg.)   0-531-15568-4 (pbk.)
    1. Space shuttles—Juvenile literature. 2. Manned space flight—Juvenile literature.
[1. Space shuttles. 2. Manned space flight. 3. Space stations.]   I. Moser, Diane, 1944-
II. Title.   III. Out of this world (Franklin Watts, Inc.)
 TL795.515 .S635 2002
 629.44'1-dc21   2001005363

Acknowledgments

We would like to thank the numerous people who contributed to *Onboard the Space Shuttle*. First of all, special appreciation goes to Melissa Palestro, science editor at Franklin Watts, who leaped courageously into the middle of this series. Appreciation also goes to Melissa Stewart, who helped shape this project's beginnings. We also would like to thank Margaret Carruthers, planetary geologist, Oxford, England, and Sam Storch of Hayden Planetarium, who reviewed the manuscript and outdid themselves by offering many great ideas for improving it. Also, thanks go to Tony Reichhardt and John Rhea, who were our editors at the former *Space World Magazine* and started us out on the fascinating journey we have taken during our years of writing about space.

Contents

Posing for the camera is the crew of the STS-99 aboard the space shuttle *Endeavour*.

Heroes
in Space

M ost of the time, astronauts get to work the same way everyone else does— traveling by car or bus, or sometimes by airplane if they have to attend a faraway meeting. But these men and women also get to commute to their jobs in a way that is far from normal. It's a long trip, but not along freeways or through city streets. Instead, these workers travel approximately 150 miles (240 kilometers) upward into the vastness of space. There they do their work aboard one of several strange vehicles called space shuttles. Part space transport, part science laboratory, and part workshop, these spacecraft—including *Columbia, Endeavour, Discovery, Atlantis,* and *Challenger* (lost in flight)—were all named after great sailing ships of the past. To the astronauts, the space shuttle is both their home and their workplace during flights that can last two weeks or more.

The astronauts onboard the space shuttles have many different jobs. Some are pilots. Others are technicians who help keep the shuttle running smoothly. Still others are scientists and researchers. Onboard the shuttle, the crew is made up of three main groups: flight crew, mission specialists, and payload specialists. It is a tight and well-organized crew of workers. It has to be. Space is not a safe and easy place to work.

The commander and the pilot make up the flight crew. They are in charge of flying the shuttle—a complicated machine made up of millions of parts. Technically, according to *NASA,* these two crew members are the astronauts—the team directly responsible for flying the shuttle. However, most people refer to the entire crew as astronauts.

Mission specialists are a team of experts who are specially trained to complete some aspect of a mission. Often they have special training to perform *EVAs* (extravehicular activities, or space walks). They also train for intricate tasks they may need to perform, such as fixing an ailing satellite or building parts of a space station.

Most payload specialists are scientists. They conduct various scientific duties including special experiments that are best done in space. For example, they study the changes in the extremely low *gravity* (*microgravity*) experienced in orbit.

Astronauts take huge risks when they go up into space. Yet these courageous crews go up again and again. This book tells the story of these heroes, who work and live onboard the space shuttle. It explores the adventures, hazards, and great beauty experienced by astronauts in Earth *orbit.* We salute these heroic people for their courage and response to challenge as they perform what many of them have called "the best job in the universe."

Andy Thomas.

Chapter 1

Opening the Space Frontier

The date is January 22, 1998. It is an exciting day for astronaut Andy Thomas —and for the rest of the STS-89 crew boarding the space shuttle *Endeavour*. This is launch day, and Thomas is one of the first astronauts to board the ship.

On this flight he is a mission specialist and is headed for the Russian space station *Mir*. By now, at age twenty-seven, he is a veteran in space, making his second shuttle launch. (Space travel is so intense that NASA considers anyone who visits space even once a veteran.) Thomas straps himself into his seat in the mid-deck area, where there are no windows. He and the two other astronauts on the mid-deck wish each other a good flight and shake hands. Then the cabin grows silent.

A deep rumble can be heard far below. The engines reach full power, and suddenly the astronauts hear the bolts that were holding the shuttle in place release. The huge spacecraft shudders with a massive vibration and a deafening roar. The cabin seems to spin as the orbiter rolls over into position for its climb. The astronauts are pressed back into their seats. Then they feel a jolt as the solid-fuel rockets drop away. *Endeavor* is traveling at thousands of feet per second, and its altitude is called out in miles from the flight deck. At 50 nautical miles (equal to 43.4 miles, or 70 km), the astronauts shake hands. By tradition, this is the border of space. They have made it. Soon their speed reaches 17,500 miles (28,000 km) per hour—orbital speed. The engines shut down and the astronauts pitch forward with the sudden sensation that they have come to a complete standstill. Of course, they haven't really stopped—they have just stopped accelerating. Now weightless, they are floating in orbit. The trip has taken only eight and a half minutes!

Opening the Space Frontier

People have been riding huge rockets into space for more than forty years, but it is still always an adventure—even for veteran astronauts. The first person to enter space was Yuri Gagarin, a Russian *cosmonaut* (or astronaut), who made the trip in 1961. It was April 12 and a lovely spring day in Earth's northern temperate zones. For Gagarin it must have been both thrilling and frightening. No other human being had ever ventured into the vacuum of space. Scientists and technicians thought they knew how to protect the human body—Gagarin wore a space suit, gloves, and a helmet. The cabin of his spacecraft was

Soviet pilot Yuri Gagarin on his way to become the first man to orbit the Earth in the Soviet spacecraft *Vostok 1.*

The space shuttle needs power to lift its huge body into space. Along with the spacecraft itself, all the cargo and people onboard also need to be lifted. The rocket is the only method anyone has used so far for reaching *escape velocity*, which is the speed needed to escape Earth's gravity and soar into space. At Earth's equator, that's more than 25,000 miles (more than 40,000 km) per hour.

What exactly is a rocket, and what makes it useful in space?

If you've ever blown up a balloon and let go of the end, you've seen one of the principles of rocket power in action. The gas inside (for example, air or helium) pushes outward equally on all sides of the balloon. The gas meets resistance in every direction but the end that contains the mouthpiece. That's why it rushes out through the mouthpiece. As the gas rushes out, it propels the balloon forward. The principle at work was first put forth by the great English physicist Isaac Newton (1643–1727). He said that for every action there is an equal and opposite reaction. The *recoil* felt by the shooter of a gun is another example of this principle, as is the method that an octopus uses to travel—by squirting out a jet of water forcefully to propel itself forward. This principle works equally well in Earth's atmosphere or in a vacuum—rockets do not need air to "push against."

The burning fuel inside rockets produces hot gases, which rush backward out of the engine, propelling the rocket forward. This process works equally as well in Earth's atmosphere as it does in the vacuum of space. For one thing, rocket engines contain everything they need to work within them. For example, liquid- and solid-fuel rockets both include a substance called an *oxidizer* that provides the oxygen required for their fuels to burn. Jet engines, however, are different than rockets. Jet engines would not work in space because they require the presence of air to produce power—they need the oxygen in the air to burn the fuel that makes them run.

supplied with oxygen under sufficient pressure to keep him from exploding. Yet no one could be sure that he would really be okay. Could his body withstand the *g-forces* as his spacecraft rushed toward the heavens? Would his eyes withstand the changes in pressure during liftoff? What would happen to the soft tissues of his brain and heart? He was the very first to try spaceflight, and this was the big test.

Once it is propelled forward, an object moving in the vacuum of space continues to move in the same direction without any power until it bumps into something else or a push causes it to move in another direction. This is another principle of motion: An object in motion stays in motion. So with no force in its way, an object will move in one direction forever. Friction, which slows down objects on Earth, does not occur in space, because there are few molecules in the vacuum of space to collide with objects. This is how we manage to send a spacecraft beyond the outer reaches of our solar system using very little fuel.

Most spacecraft have two *rocket thrusters*, one on each side. A rocket thruster produces thrust, or push, in a particular direction. In order to turn the spacecraft, only one of the thrusters might be used. In order for it to proceed straight ahead, both could be turned on at once, at equal levels of thrust.

In this artist's impression of the launch of an Ariane 5 rocket, you can see there are two large, solid rocket *boosters* connected to the main body of the rocket.

A lot of problems could have developed, and no one really knew what might go wrong. Luckily, Gagarin returned home safely.

A few weeks later, on May 5, 1961, American astronaut Alan Shepard became the second human to enter space. However, in terms of the danger of his mission, he might as well have been the first into space, since he had little or no information about Gagarin's flight. He knew only that Gagarin had made his way back to Earth and lived to smile and wave at the crowds afterward.

Actually, Gagarin had more problems descending back into Earth's atmosphere than most people knew at the time. Back then, Russia was part of a coalition of nations known as the Union of Soviet Socialist Republics (USSR, or Soviet Union). Spaceflight began during a period known as the Cold War—a time when the USSR had strained relations with many countries, including the United States. To promote an image of success, the Soviet government kept a tight control on all news, and spaceflight was no exception. Gagarin's trip to space was reported as having gone perfectly.

Years later, when the Cold War was over and the Soviet government had been dismantled, the world found out that Gagarin's return to Earth from space did not go as smoothly as everyone was led to believe. As the braking rocket began to slow the spacecraft's descent, a wild spin began. The spacecraft separated from the rocket later than it was supposed to, and the capsule threatened to go out of control. Luckily, Gagarin made it back to Earth safely.

Von Braun's Vision

One of the first great rocket pioneers was Wernher von Braun, the man who oversaw the designing, building, and testing of all the rockets used in the early days of the U.S. space program.

Von Braun came to the United States in 1945. He had been building rockets since he was a boy in the 1920s. He grew up in Germany, where he was an active member of a club of men who were fascinated with rockets and the idea of space travel. At the time no one knew a lot about how to build a rocket, and most people thought travel in space was just a fantasy for dreamers.

In the early 1930s, though, the German army offered von Braun a job in a new rocket program it had just established. Von Braun thought it would be a great opportunity to develop rockets and learn how they worked. However, the job turned out to have a sinister objective that was probably unknown to von Braun at first. By 1939 Germany had attacked Poland, and World War II had begun. Before the end of the war, German rockets were destroying towns and villages throughout Europe. Many rockets fell in populated areas of London. People and homes were destroyed. The rockets were the ones designed and tested by von Braun and his team of rocket experts.

After the war ended in 1945, von Braun and his team found a way to continue building their knowledge and ability—and, ultimately, to use their talents for more positive goals. The U.S. Army recognized that these men had valuable skills. More than one hundred top German rocket experts, including von Braun, received invitations to continue their work on rockets in the United States. Most of them accepted.

During the next twelve years, von Braun's team improved its rocket designs. The team members tested and experimented, and by 1957 they had a rocket they were sure could venture into space. However, Cold War politics kept them from trying it out. The U.S. government wanted to send a rocket to space but did not want to appear dependent on the team of German engineers. So it looked to other teams for rockets to send into space.

Meanwhile, the Soviet Union was doing similar research. On October 4, 1957, the Soviet Union sent the first satellite, *Sputnik I,*

Sputnik I, the first Russian satellite to enter space, displayed on a stand shortly before its launch on October 4, 1957.

into orbit atop a huge rocket. Now it was too late for the United States to be first to achieve this. Still, the U.S. government did not turn to the Army's rocket, which had been developed by von Braun and his team. So after the launch of *Sputnik*, the U.S. Navy was ordered to hurry completion of its own rocket, *Vanguard*. It would carry a tiny satellite that would help prove to the world that the United States was equal to the Soviet Union in both technology and power.

Just over two months later, on December 6, 1957, *Vanguard* was ready to go. As it stood on the launch pad, American hopes soared high. However, rockets are complex, and especially in the early days, they didn't always work perfectly. This was one of those times for *Vanguard*. Just as the rocket began to lift from the launch pad, it suddenly lost power, sank back to the launch pad, and exploded. It was a huge disappointment for the American public, as well as the politicians, scientists, and engineers looking forward to the launch.

Now the situation was even more urgent. The United States needed a success, and President Eisenhower finally turned to von Braun and his team for help. They were ready. On January 31, 1958, their *Jupiter C* rocket (which was renamed *Juno*, perceived as a gentler name) lifted off and rose steadily toward space. It released a small "passenger" into orbit, a scientific satellite named *Explorer 1*. America had its success! (Two months later, the next *Jupiter C* failed, though—showing that no one's rockets were perfect.)

From these beginnings, von Braun and his team built a series of powerful engines. These were the rockets that launched the first U.S. astronauts into space during Project Mercury and the daring pioneer spacewalkers of the Project Gemini missions. Finally, they carried the

Apollo astronauts to the Moon. Today, the United States and the world owe their toehold in space to the work done by this group of talented engineers from the mid-1930s to the 1970s.

The Practical View

On May 5, 1961, Alan Shepard became the first American to enter space. Within three weeks, President John F. Kennedy set forth a monumental challenge to Americans: to go to the Moon within the next ten years. It was an extraordinary goal—a "new frontier" no one had ever attempted to reach. It would be the job of the newly formed U.S. space agency, the National Aeronautics and Space Administration (NASA), to figure out how to make it happen. It was a thrilling goal and a politically important job. Kennedy's challenge to the American people also became a challenge to the Soviet Union's space agency. Who would get there first? Whoever won the race to the Moon, both countries reasoned, would win the world's respect as the more powerful and technologically advanced nation.

Within NASA, debates raged among the officials, engineers, and designers. What was the best way to get there safely and quickly? To von Braun, only one answer made sense: build a rocket that could lift materials and workers into orbit. Then build a space station, one piece at a time, in space. This could be achieved by constructing a reusable spacecraft that could shuttle people and supplies back and forth between Earth and the space station. From the space station, missions to the Moon could be launched easily and economically. The space station would act as a wayside stopover—a place to get ready for the journey. An emergency vehicle could be kept there to rescue endangered astronauts.

Later, the space station could be a launch site for journeys to Mars. It was the best, most practical, most economical, and safest way to go.

Unfortunately, it would have taken many years to learn how to build a space station while in orbit. In 1961 no one had the skill to build things in space. Astronauts and cosmonauts had not even made the first space walks yet. (Those took place in 1963, and even then, the astronauts still had a lot to learn.) The first reusable spacecraft, the space shuttle, would not make its first space flight until 1981. And not until the twenty-first century would U.S. astronauts have full access to a large space station where they could live and work for months at a time and then travel back to Earth aboard a reusable spacecraft. Back in 1961 a space station big enough to fit von Braun's vision was too difficult a project and would have taken far too much time for a nation eager to win a "space race." Von Braun had a good idea, but he was overruled.

So, during the first two decades of the U.S. space program, every spacebound mission required a rocket that could not be reused. From the first rocket used to lift a satellite toward space to the last Moon landing in 1972—and, after that, the Skylab missions in 1973–1974 and the joint U.S.-Soviet Apollo-Soyuz mission in 1975—these giant beasts thundered into the skies. They did their jobs and did them well, but there was no way to reuse them. The rockets that took astronauts to the Moon were enormous Saturn V rockets that made all the rockets built before them look like toothpicks. They were powerful, but they were expensive.

At the same time, the United States was thinking about another way of getting to space: using a winged spacecraft that could fly in

Since the beginning of NASA's human spaceflight programs in the late 1950s—and even before that—many young men and women have dreamed of going to space.

The first seven U.S. astronauts—known as the Mercury Seven—will always be remembered for their heroism during those first voyages into space. Their names reside in the memories of all Americans who witnessed those exciting days and everyone who yearns to go to space. Three were Air Force captains: L. Gordon Cooper Jr., Virgil "Gus" Grissom, and Donald K. "Deke" Slayton. The first to orbit Earth, Lieutenant Colonel John H. Glenn Jr., was the only representative from the U.S. Marines. The remaining three were from the Navy: Lieutenant M. Scott Carpenter and Lieutenant Comman-

ders Walter M. Schirra Jr., and Alan B. Shepard Jr. Of those first seven chosen astronauts, everyone flew alone in a capsule, except Deke Slayton, who was held back for medical reasons. (Finally, he did have his chance to fly in space when he commanded the U.S. team in the Apollo-Soyuz mission in 1975. It was a goodwill mission that docked a U.S. Apollo spacecraft with a Soviet Soyuz spacecraft. It was the first docking between spacecraft from the two countries—a forerunner of U.S. space shuttle dockings with the Russian space station *Mir* in the late 1990s.)

Today, some astronauts—especially pilots—still enter the astronaut corps from a military background. When NASA chooses shuttle astronauts, though, academic background often outweighs flight experience. Many candidates have doc-

Earth's *atmosphere*, exit to space, and then fly back to Earth again. Early test pilots broke records and soared to unheard-of altitudes in the X-series of jet planes from the 1940s to the 1960s. Chuck Yeager broke the sound barrier in the X-1 in 1947. By 1961 test pilots had pushed the X-15 experimental jet to Mach 5.27, more than five times the

torates in one of the natural sciences, medicine, or engineering. NASA selected the first group of shuttle astronaut candidates in 1978. These candidates underwent intensive training to qualify for assignment to a shuttle flight crew. All thirty five who started training finished by August 1979. Of those, twenty were scientists—payload specialists—and the other fifteen were pilots. The group included six women and four minorities—two groups who previously had not been included among U.S. astronaut crews. Those thirty-five men and women were the vanguard of a growing pool of shuttle astronauts. Further selections followed in 1980, 1984, 1985, 1987, 1990, 1992, 1995, and 1996.

Future astronauts will face ever more complex challenges as the construction of the International Space Station (ISS) continues. The ISS is a joint enterprise, shared with international partners including Japan, Canada, Russia, and the European Space Agency (ESA). With the ongoing construction and the future establishment of space station research missions, the need for more astronauts is now greater than ever. NASA needs people with specialized qualifications—and the ability to work for extended time periods and in close quarters with coworkers from varied backgrounds. NASA now accepts applications continuously for the Astronaut Candidate Program. Selection of candidates takes place about every two years. Civilians can apply at any time, but military candidates are chosen through the parent service structure.

speed of sound, and were soaring to the edges of space. A project called DynaSoar was in the works, which was intended to become a U.S. Air Force military spacecraft. None of these experimental aircraft ever entered space, but something else began to develop slowly during this time—an idea that became the space shuttle.

Every space shuttle now has the same design, which
looks like a cross between an airplane and a rocket.

Chapter 2

A Workhorse
for Space

Early in the U.S. space program's history, it became obvious that NASA needed a reusable launch vehicle and spacecraft. Early technology required building completely new rockets and spacecraft before every launch. Imagine throwing away the family car after every trip to the supermarket or the shopping mall! Even today, many satellites are launched by "expendable" rockets. That is, after the rocket is used, it is thrown away and either becomes "space garbage" in orbit or falls back through the atmosphere into Earth's oceans. It can never be used again—it's just trash. The spacecraft carried to space atop these rockets were not reused, either. No spacecraft used in any of the early human spaceflight programs could ever be used twice. The space capsules used by Gagarin and Shepard parachuted back to Earth. Gagarin dropped down onto the expanses of land in western Russia, near the Volga River. Shepard splashed down in the Atlantic Ocean. Once they had safely landed, their spacecraft never returned to space.

Unfortunately, this practice was not very economical. Spacecraft and rockets cost a lot of money to build, and so the idea of reusing some of them held tremendous attraction. As long ago as 1933, Austrian rocket designer Eugen Sänger designed a rocket-space-plane with wings. He called his winged "reusable space transporter" the *Silver Bird.* By the late 1960s, the idea of building a reusable space vehicle was actively being discussed. NASA and the U.S. Congress became interested, and by 1972—the year the last Apollo mission went to the Moon—a decision was made. On January 5, President Richard M. Nixon and NASA chief administrator James C. Fletcher announced that the space shuttle program had received final approval. The space shuttle would become the primary U.S. link with space—a cargo ship used to launch both spacecraft and satellites into space. It could also serve to carry scientific experiments into orbit. It would revolutionize travel to near space, Nixon said, by making it routine.

First Flights

The first shuttle tests took place from February to November 1977 at Dryden Flight Research Facility in California. A special test version of the shuttle, the space shuttle *Enterprise,* first underwent tests of its ability to taxi on the ground, brake, and maneuver. Then it was flown first pilotless and then with pilots onboard in tests atop a Boeing 747. The shuttle actually rode "piggyback" on the big jet. Then astronauts took it on several free-flight tests within Earth's atmosphere. These tests showed that *Enterprise* could fly in Earth's atmosphere and land like an airplane—except that it did not have *power-gliding flight* (and it still doesn't have powered flight). This big vehicle had wings and landing wheels like a plane, and it could land on a runway like a plane, but it couldn't take off like a plane. It needed rockets to act as boosters. It was NASA's compromise for getting into space and back more economically and efficiently. Like all compromises, it had both its good and bad points.

The following year, *Enterprise* was modified and then traveled to Marshall Spaceflight Center in Huntsville, Alabama. There, the big vehicle underwent more tests while joined to external booster rockets and a fuel tank.

Enterprise then went to Kennedy Space Center (KSC), where more tests were performed. By 1979 hopes were high. The first shuttle spaceflight appeared to be just around the corner.

A "Stickler" Stops the Show

One big problem had slowed down the progress, though. NASA continued to fly the space shuttle orbiters piggyback on the big 747 aircraft to transport them from one location to another. The orbiter *Columbia* was traveling on just such a trip in 1979 when 40 percent of its protective tiles fell off. These specially designed ceramic tiles were supposed to protect the shuttle's exterior from the extreme, fiery heat it would have to endure during a mission when it reentered Earth's atmosphere from orbit. The shuttle's underside and nose would have to withstand temperatures reaching as high as 2,300 to 2,600 degrees Fahrenheit (1,260 to 1,425 degrees Celsius). This situation posed a real danger to the crew and the shuttle. Replacing the tiles was also costly. NASA put the shuttle program on hold for two years while researchers studied the problem. Finally, they came up with new designs for the tiles that improved their durability and their ability to stick to the shuttle. Finally, NASA gave the go-ahead for launch.

Space at Last!

On April 12, 1981, the orbiter *Columbia* stood on the launch pad, pointing skyward and ready for countdown. It was twenty years to the day since Gagarin's first spaceflight. This would be the first mission for the Space Transportation System (STS), as the space shuttle is officially known. Its glistening white body looked like an enormous airplane standing on end, while its great, planelike structure caused a sense of awe in observers. A huge liquid-fuel engine flanked by two solid-fuel rockets rode piggyback, the first time liquid and solid-fuel rockets were used together to launch astronauts into space. After several delays, the countdown concluded, the engines roared, and *Columbia* climbed up and up, the rocket engines falling away as their fuel was used. Finally, the huge white bird ascended into orbit.

Columbia landed two days later, touching down like an oversize airplane at Edwards Air Force Base in California. Overall, everything had gone extremely well. However, NASA officials still worried about the tiles: Sixteen of them had fallen off and 148 were damaged. But that situation wasn't really dangerous—out of 28,000 tiles, there were still enough to do the job. And overall, the shuttle design worked well. The first truly reusable piloted U.S. spacecraft was finally in business.

As for the stalwart space shuttle *Enterprise,* it was never equipped to travel in space. It was only a test vehicle. So once all the testing was completed, *Enterprise* went on tour—to the Paris, France, Air Show, as

The *Enterprise* lands during a test flight.

well as to Germany, Italy, England, and Canada in 1983 and to the 1984 World's Fair in New Orleans, Louisiana. The following year, NASA transferred the *Enterprise* to the Smithsonian Institution's National Air and Space Museum in Washington, D.C.

Space Shuttle Basics

The space shuttle is made up of four parts. The reusable, winged spacecraft called the orbiter is the heart of the system. At launch it is mounted piggyback on the second main part—a huge, external fuel tank that holds liquid hydrogen (the fuel) and liquid oxygen (to burn the fuel) for the shuttle's main engines. The third and fourth part, the two solid-fuel booster rockets mounted on each side of the external tank, complete the launch equipment.

The mammoth external tank, which dominates the launch pad view during liftoff from KSC in Florida is 27.49 feet (8.38 meters) wide and 154.2 feet (47 m) long. The entire system weighs 4.4 million pounds (2 million kilograms) and stands 184 feet (56 m) high on the launch pad. At a typical launch, the shuttle's main engines ignite about six seconds before liftoff. The solid-fuel booster rockets ignite at T = 0, the final moment of countdown. Finally, the bolts that hold the shuttle in place are released. Liftoff occurs about two and a half seconds later. As the shuttle roars skyward, huge billows of white smoke surround it as the two boosters add their thrust to the rumbling lift of the main engines. About two minutes after liftoff, the boosters are jettisoned, or released, and they fall away as the external tank-orbiter combination continues toward space. (The solid-fuel rockets can be collected from where they land in the ocean and can be refilled.) By the time the orbiter is near the *velocity,* or speed, required to reach

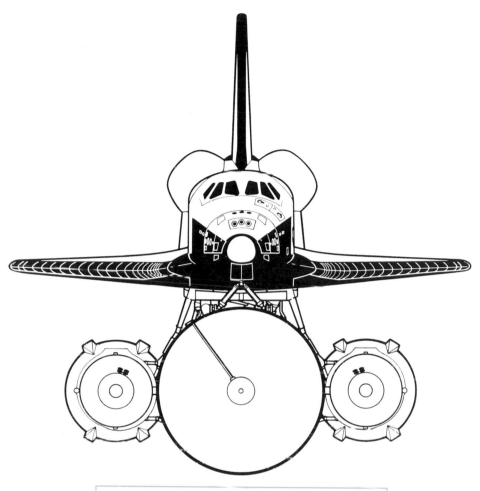

In this view looking down on the space shuttle on the launch pad, the large circle at the bottom is the external tank, with a solid-fuel rocket on each side.

orbit, it has used up all the fuel in the external tank. The empty tank drops away and disintegrates as it falls through the atmosphere toward Earth.

During launch, the shuttle functions as a rocket does, but now, without the external tank and booster rockets, the orbiter becomes a spacecraft. It will not use its main engines again during the mission.

Later, at the end of the mission, it becomes a *hypersonic* glider—traveling faster than five times the speed of sound. At this last stage, it looks more like a jet airplane than a rocket.

The Promises

During the program's first four years of spaceflight, the space shuttle had always done its job. Like many other U.S. science and technology programs, though, it suffered from constant budget cuts. In the late 1970s and early 1980s, as NASA tried to get the shuttle's millions of complex parts to work together, less and less money was available to the organization. Whenever the budget was cut, progress was slowed. Yet at the same time, impossible promises were made to the funding agencies and the American public. Nixon's vision of routine transportation to near space had not really come true, and probably never will. Space is a dangerous environment, and getting there requires complex technology. Still, NASA promised that space shuttle flights would take place with greater frequency, even though constant delays were the rule. By 1985 there were four orbiters, and three of them flew a total of nine missions. Even more missions were planned for 1986.

The shuttle's early problems had brought about criticism of the entire program. Everyone remembered the falling tiles. Very few people seemed to recognize how useful the shuttle program had become, not realizing the growing uses for the communications satellites, mapping satellites, and weather satellites launched by the shuttles. Within the space program, some critics thought money should be devoted to planetary and scientific research done by robot spacecraft instead of the shuttle program. Others thought NASA should pursue the idea of building a spacecraft that could both take off and land like an airplane.

Meanwhile, to meet demands, schedules were tightened—but the reduced budget did not allow for the kind of double and triple safeguards NASA had learned to require. NASA and everyone else were beginning to believe that shuttle flights into space could become regularly scheduled and routine. Eventually, the time and money pressure took its toll in the worst possible way—a fatal flight.

The crew of the space shuttle *Challenger*. Front row, from left to right: Michael Smith, Francis Scobee, Ronald McNair. Back row, from left to right: Ellison Onizuka, Christa McAuliffe, Gregory Jarvis, Judith Resnik.

Chapter 3

"Routine" Becomes Catastrophe

On January 28, 1986, as the twenty-fifth space shuttle mission began, a tragedy occurred. Just seventy-three seconds after liftoff, smoke began shooting out of the cluster of giant rocket engines that lifted the space shuttle *Challenger* skyward. A giant explosion followed. *Challenger* broke into pieces and fell to the ocean. The orbiter was lost and every member of the seven-person crew died. Known as flight STS-51L, it was the last shuttle mission for more than a year and a half. Lost were Francis R. "Dick" Scobee, Michael J. Smith, Judith A. Resnik, Ronald E. McNair, Ellison S. Onizuka, Gregory B. Jarvis, and Christa McAuliffe. McAuliffe was an elementary-school teacher who had been chosen to become the "first teacher in space," and thousands of schoolchildren were watching the launch on classroom televisions.

Pictures taken shortly after the STS-51L rockets fired showed a small puff of black smoke coming from the lower end of the right rocket booster. This was a spot where O-shaped rings (known as O-rings) were supposed to seal a joint. However, January 28 was an ice-cold morning on the Florida coast. Icicles hung from the shuttle as it stood preparing for liftoff. Investigators concluded that the cold weather had made the rings so brittle that they no longer held their seal. The investigators watched the films of the disaster over and over. Right after liftoff, the smoke seemed to disappear. The engine heat probably softened the O-rings enough to reseal the joint. But the wind was brisk and *Challenger* was buffeted sharply as it rose toward space. The shuttle was built to weather the sea winds, though, and usually it would have taken the beating well—but not this time. The already damaged seals apparently broke again, and this time the rupture didn't reseal. A flame burst from the joint, and the rocket fuel ignited in a nightmare of fire and smoke. The rest is tragic history.

Further investigation showed that production crews were under too great a time pressure. As a result, not enough attention had been given to quality control. Workers had noticed problems with the O-rings long before *Challenger* reached the launch pad and had reported them. Yet officials had given the go-ahead to launch the flight. No one wanted to delay the schedule, and the problems had gone unsolved.

A lot had to change before the shuttle program could return to space. Better management, clearer communication, and absolute concern for quality had to be reinstilled. Until then, no one could guarantee that the shuttle would ever be safe.

The launch pad on January 28, 1986, before the launch of the space shuttle *Challenger*.

Around the world, billions of people witnessed the accident on television and mourned the *Challenger* crew.

An intense investigation was launched to uncover the reasons for the accident. During this time the American human presence in space was noticeably lacking. It remained this way until 1988, when NASA was satisfied that the problem was solved. Only the brilliant photos and details returned to Earth from *Voyager 2* as it flew by the faraway planet Uranus testified to the American ability to make things work, and work well, in space. Most people neglected to think how greatly we already relied on space activities—especially the ever-busy satellites in the skies, which watched the weather, monitored the changes in our planet, relayed communications, connected databases, and so on.

As a result of the investigating team's findings, a major reorganization of shuttle management took place. Stringent, new quality controls went into effect, and many technical changes were made. NASA also created a new Office of Safety, Reliability, Maintainability, and Quality Assurance. NASA was determined to make every effort to prevent another loss like *Challenger*. Many important missions were delayed. Commercial satellites had to find another way to reach orbit. Time passed. NASA was not going to return the shuttle to space without having full confidence in its reliability. *Challenger* had served as a tragic reminder that the voyage to space is risky and potentially dangerous. It was a reminder no one was likely to forget.

Return to Flight

Finally, on September 29, 1988, the space shuttle returned to space with the launch of STS-26 *Discovery*. Many successful flights followed. Many of these missions were sent into space to begin preparations for

Space Shuttle

Vital Statistics

WEIGHT AT LAUNCH	4.5 million pounds (2 million kg)
HEIGHT	184.2 feet (56.1 m)
CARGO TO ORBIT	63,500 pounds (28,803 kg)
ORBITER WIDTH (WING TIP TO WING TIP)	78.06 feet (23.79 m)
ORBITER LENGTH	122.2 feet (37.2 m)
ORBITER FLEET	*Atlantis* *Challenger* (exploded 73 seconds after liftoff) *Columbia* *Discovery* *Endeavour* *Enterprise* (Earthbound test vehicle)

the construction of the International Space Station (ISS). Von Braun's dream was slowly beginning to become reality.

Meanwhile, the shuttle crews also launched numerous satellites, including the *Hubble Space Telescope,* which payload specialists placed in orbit from the shuttle bay in 1990. When it proved to have a flawed mirror, *Endeavour* astronauts became heroes in 1993 by performing an EVA repair mission to install a set of corrective lenses on it.

Dozens of scientific missions have also flown since 1988, including numerous Spacelab and SPACEHAB missions. (Spacelab is a reusable laboratory designed by the European Space Agency to fit into the shuttle bay. SPACEHAB is a commercial company that supplies specialized containers that fit in the shuttle bay for various kinds of

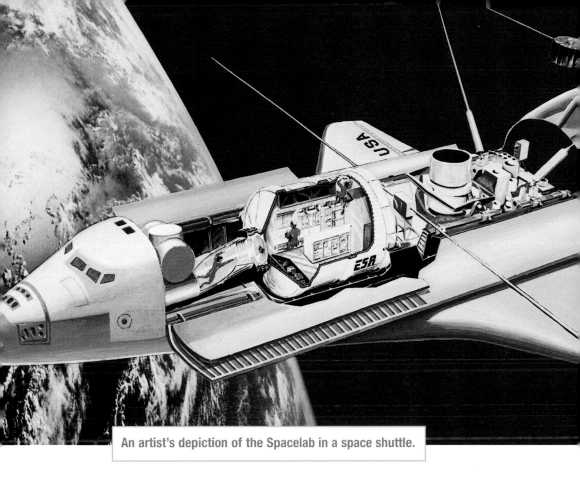

An artist's depiction of the Spacelab in a space shuttle.

projects.) The experiments included tests of the effects of microgravity on various materials, life-science experiments, solar studies, space physics experiments, and astrophysics research.

Today, as the ISS grows, the shuttle has begun to serve its original purpose: a shuttle, or taxi, between Earth and a space station. The brave men and women who fly the shuttle and live and work in the ISS have begun to turn science fiction into reality—creating a permanent, international presence in space.

Astronaut Curtis L. Brown Jr., mission commander, operates controls on the flight deck of the space shuttle *Discovery*.

Chapter 4

Living in Space

NASA astronauts have continued working high above Earth's surface in numerous missions in Earth orbit. From the start, being an astronaut has meant working in space, not just piloting a spacecraft. Astronauts and other specialists try out new hardware and test the effects of microgravity to see how substances, people, and other living things react when Earth's normal gravity is not present. Astronauts have also launched satellites, made important repairs to objects in space, and built structures. Since the 1980s they have done most of this work aboard one of NASA's space shuttles.

Inside the Space Shuttle

Inside, the space shuttle has a pressurized forward compartment that is divided into two decks. The upper deck is the flight deck, where the commander and pilot and often a mission specialist operate the shuttle controls and watch the displays on the control panels. This area has big windows, and one of the favorite pastimes of astronauts onboard is to go up to the flight deck and view Earth from there. Astronauts may see shimmering *aurorae* over the poles at night or the movement of clouds across the continents and oceans. Astronaut crews have taken many photographs from this vantage point, providing us with an entirely new and breathtaking perspective of our planet.

The lower deck is called the mid-deck. It is where most of the crew sleeps. The galley, or kitchen, is located in one corner of this area. Exercise equipment and laboratory experiments may also be located there. The flight deck and the mid-deck are the only areas supplied with air and pressure. To explore any other part of the shuttle, astronauts have to put on space suits to provide them with air to breathe, a pressurized environment like Earth's (so that they don't explode), and protection against the extreme cold and heat found in the environment of space.

A hatch from the mid-deck leads to the shuttle payload bay, also known as the cargo bay. The hatch area provides a special airtight passageway, or air lock, between the pressurized cabin and the airlessness of the bay. Here, astronauts about to perform an EVA put on their space suits and helmets and allow their bodies to adjust to the oxygen they will be breathing while outside. Then they pass through the hatch to the cargo bay.

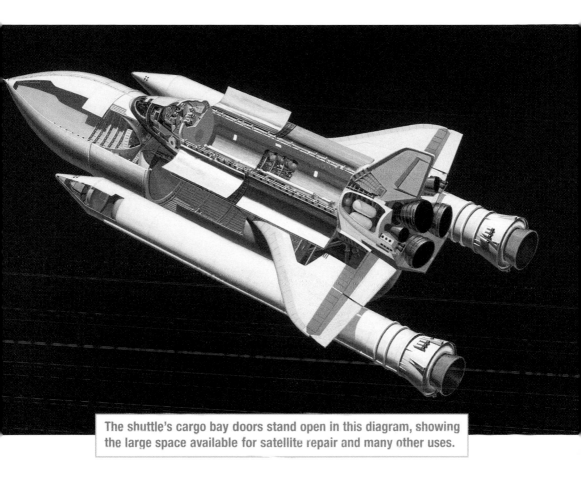

The shuttle's cargo bay doors stand open in this diagram, showing the large space available for satellite repair and many other uses.

The cargo bay in the shuttle's midsection is, by far, the largest compartment in the shuttle. The enormous doors of the bay are often opened as soon as the shuttle reaches orbit. Inside the bay, the shuttle may carry a satellite or spacecraft to deploy, a satellite it has retrieved, or laboratory experiments. The cargo bay sometimes carries an insulated module called the Spacelab, which provides a reusable laboratory space for carrying out extensive experiments. The first Spacelab flew in 1983, and many have flown since then. A Spacelab module flew aboard STS-90 in April 1998 for a mission called Neurolab. During this mission, payload specialists conducted physiology experiments to investigate the effects of weightlessness, especially on the nervous system. The effects of microgravity are always a major concern and interest for those working in space. No one is sure exactly what all the effects of working and living in space for extended time periods may be. These are important to understand when planning long stays on the space station or missions to faraway destinations, such as Mars.

The shuttle's large main engines are housed at the rear section of the shuttle. The orbital maneuvering system is also located in this area. This system allows the commander and pilot to change the shuttle's orbit around Earth so that the shuttle can rendezvous, or meet, with satellites and other spacecraft. This is essential for retrieving and repairing satellites, which is one of the shuttle crew's most exciting and important jobs.

Moving Around

Getting used to the dramatic change in gravity is probably the most challenging adjustment for the astronauts. Many movements that people take for granted are not at all easy to perform in microgravity. One astronaut explains that his first impression of microgravity was that it was like being in a swimming pool—only air is much thinner than water and is easier to move through. Astronauts float everywhere. Handrails and handholds are the mainstays of shuttle life on the mid-deck, in the payload bay, and on the flight deck. Foot restraints are installed wherever an astronaut might need to stand, work, or accomplish a task. Otherwise, feet don't stay on the floor. Every movement sends an astronaut drifting off in another direction. Rookie astronauts say they find themselves moving very slowly at first—not because it is hard to move, but because it's too easy to move. Once a crew member begins moving in one direction, the movement continues until something gets in the way or he or she finds some way to stop the movement.

Eating

The shuttle's galley, or kitchen, is a small area in the corner of the middeck. There is no refrigerator or freezer onboard, so most food is freeze-dried like camping food and is vacuum-packed inside plastic containers so that it will keep from spoiling for a long time. Soft food is stored in tubes and can be squeezed out. Liquids are stored in packages with attached straws that are similar to the drinks that get packed in school lunches. A station in the galley has a cold- and hot-water supply. Astronauts add water to their dried food through special ports in the containers. Labels tell the astronauts exactly how much water to add and how long to wait before eating the meal. Foods can also be heated in a special forced-air convection oven. Foot restraints in the galley make cooking much easier. Astronauts find using the oven or getting water easier to accomplish when their feet are held down and their movements are stabilized.

Snacks can be chosen from trays covered with netting that prevents the items from floating away. Sandwiches are usually made with flour tortillas instead of bread, since bread gets moldy quickly and is crumbly. Packed with nitrogen in plastic bags, tortillas can last as long as six months. Astronaut Bill McArthur created a special space breakfast sandwich made of two tortillas, a sausage patty, scrambled eggs, and

cheese spread. McArthur says the concoction is tasty and also allows him to consume several foods at the same time. Of course, they tend to float separately if you don't hold them together!

Puddings and liquids get squeezed out of tubes or straws and directed toward the mouth. Astronauts quickly become adept at catching droplets in midair and have even been known to play with them.

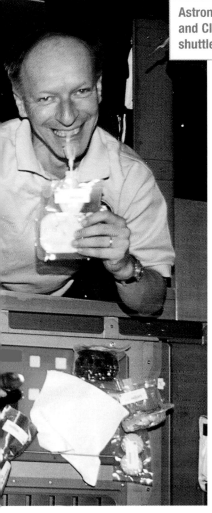

Among the favorite foods onboard the shuttle are shrimp cocktail, potatoes au gratin, chocolate pudding, dried beef, trail mix, butter cookies, granola bars, cashews, macadamia nuts, almonds, orange-mango drink, and lemonade. You may have noticed that not very many of the "favorite foods" require preparation! That may be because each astronaut usually prepares his or her own food. After the items are prepared, the astronauts attach the containers to their trays with fasteners. (Remember—everything floats in space!) Each astronaut has a personal set of silverware, including a knife, a fork, two spoons (large and small), and a pair of scissors for cutting open the plastic packages. Then each person cleans up after him- or herself.

Exercising

Weightlessness makes life easy—lifting massive loads is easy. However, bones lose calcium and strength with lack of exercise, and muscles grow flabby. The most important muscle—the heart—can become considerably weakened in space. So the astronauts' day usually includes an exercise period of at least thirty minutes (or longer if exercise forms a part of an experiment that is being conducted).

On Earth, gravity causes blood to pool in the legs, and exercise forces blood through the veins back to the heart, where it is pumped out to the arteries. In space, blood and other fluids in the body are no longer drawn downward by gravity, so fluids build up in the upper body, face, and head. (That's why astronauts usually seem to have puffy faces in space.)

The body tries to adapt to the change in gravity by regulating the amount of fluid it retains. So it excretes the excess fluid, and within three days in space, the fluid in the body is reduced by about one-third. The lack of blood and fluid caused by this adaptation can create disturbances when the astronaut returns to Earth and endures the stress of our home planet's normal gravity, such as lightheadedness and fainting.

Cardiovascular exercise (stimulating the heart, lungs, and related system of veins and arteries) is a prime concern of astronauts, as it can prevent fainting caused by fluid loss. So most shuttle flights carry a bicycle machine attached to an *ergometer* for measuring the amount of exercise done. Installing the bicycle and ergometer is usually one of the first jobs done by a crew once the shuttle is in orbit. The crew decides where to put it, depending on the payload and other factors, such as the number of shifts—since some payloads are carried in the mid-deck and multiple shifts may mean that someone is exercising while someone else is trying to sleep in the same area. The crew may decide to install the bike on the flight deck or the mid-deck. A treadmill is sometimes used, but vibrations from the treadmill may disturb microgravity experiments that are in progress. Astronauts also flex their muscles

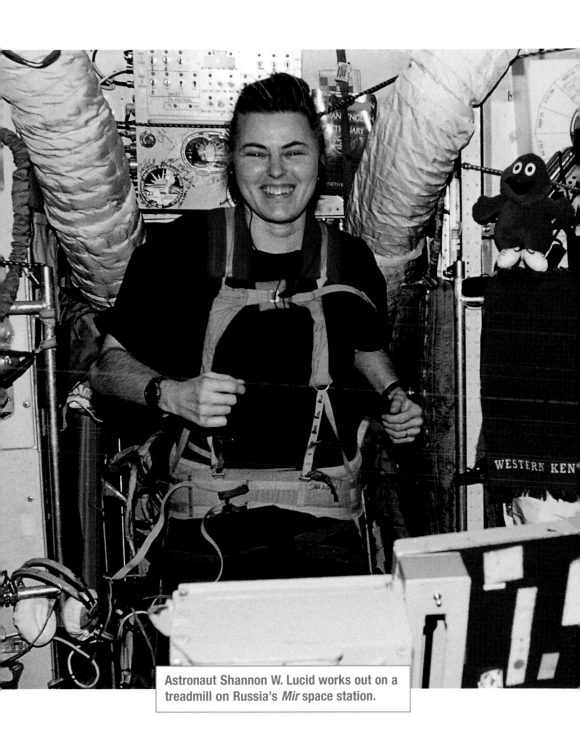

Astronaut Shannon W. Lucid works out on a treadmill on Russia's *Mir* space station.

Everything is weightless in space, and fluids are no exception. Drops of fluid released into the air don't fall or pool; they just float freely. The normal effects of *surface tension* are still in effect, though. Surface tension occurs at the interface between two different phases of matter—for example, water (liquid) and air (gas). At this interface the surface of the water seems to act as though it were "thicker" than the rest of the water on the interior. For example, if you're careful, you can fill a glass with water slightly above the rim without spilling any. Water inside a straw or tube also seems to "crawl" up the inside of the cylinder. In space, the forces of surface tension remain in effect, controlling the circumference of a drop of liquid so that it forms a perfect sphere. This is a little like a bead of water on a freshly waxed car, except that in space it remains suspended instead of clinging to any surface. For similar reasons, when an astronaut sweats during a workout in space, perspiration doesn't stream down his or her body the way it does on Earth. It just beads up. So an exercising astronaut usually keeps a towel nearby to wipe off the perspiration as it forms.

by stretching bungee cords, which are similar to large rubber bands. These exercises help to strengthen muscles and prevent some loss of muscle tone.

Sleeping

Sleeping arrangements on the shuttle are not much like home. Some astronauts just float freely in the mid-deck area. Their relaxed arms float loosely in front of them. Most crew members, though, sleep in sleeping bags. These sleeping bags are not designed for warmth, however. Their main purpose is to hold the sleeper in one place. An astronaut might attach his or her sleeping bag to a wall sideways or vertically. Position doesn't matter since there is no "up" or "down" in space. The pull of gravity creates that sensation, and you cannot feel the effect of gravity when you're flying 150 to 375 miles (250 to 600 km) above

Astronaut Kevin R. Kregel demonstrates the sleep restraints on the space shuttle *Discovery*'s mid-deck.

Earth's surface. Because the sleeping bags are not insulated, astronauts often sleep in warm clothes. They may also put masks over their eyes, since lights may remain on. Some people don't like the sensation of having their legs and arms floating freely, so they fasten them loosely. Some astronauts also like to fasten objects to their heads or backs to simulate the pressure of a pillow or mattress.

Shuttle crews sometimes work on a double shift, with round-the-clock activity divided between the two halves of the crew. Half of the crew will sleep while the other half works, often doing activities in the mid-deck area. On these missions the shuttle is usually outfitted with bunks. These look a lot like sardine cans attached in a stack along one wall. Each bunk is outfitted with a sleeping bag and a sliding door that can be used to shut out the light and noise.

Where's the Restroom?

Since everything floats in space, you can imagine what would happen if the space shuttle had ordinary restroom facilities. In the restroom, as in the galley, keeping both solid and liquid matter under control is a prime concern. The space shuttle has only one bathroom, which is separated from the rest of the mid-deck by a curtain. It can be used only in space. It contains a special toilet that operates like a vacuum, pulling air and solid waste material into a sealed storage area. Astronauts remove the tight-fitting lid before using the emptied toilet. For liquid waste, astronauts use the urinal hose, which is a long, gray tube. Each astronaut has a personal urinal funnel that attaches to the hose. Dispensers on the walls provide moist and dry wipes for cleaning up.

Hitting the Showers

Space shuttle astronauts don't even have the luxury of a cold shower, much less a hot, steamy bath. So they take sponge baths and wash their hair with rinseless shampoos designed for hospital patients who can't get out of bed.

Each astronaut has a personal hygiene kit (PHK) that contains the items he or she has chosen for the trip. Toothbrushing functions about

This toilet (left) and shower (right) are under
development and will be on future space stations.

the same as it does on Earth, and most astronauts use their favorite brands of toothpaste. Astronauts who want to shave either use electric razors (which work just fine in space) or disposable razors and shaving cream (which is harder to clean up). Making sure things don't float away is always a challenge. Most astronauts attach their PHKs to fasteners on the mid-deck wall while using the items inside. They may also store items they plan to use, such as towels, in their pockets.

Speaking of looking after one's appearance, everyone enjoys fuller-bodied hair in space! The lack of gravity means that hair does not lie flat, so long hair floats away from the body to its full length, giving astronauts a truly "big hair" look. Most long-haired astronauts use ties or rubber bands to keep their hair from floating around while they work.

Housekeeping

One of the biggest housekeeping problems in space is the presence of dust or crumbs. Without gravity they don't ever come to rest and float freely into machinery and equipment, up astronauts' nostrils, and even into their eyes. One of the most common jobs for an onboard medical officer is removing specks of dust from astronauts' eyes—and these officers soon learn to do it quickly and effectively. Filters on all the equipment have to be vacuumed several times a day to free them of collected dust that has been sucked in. NASA planners usually try to keep floating droplets, dust, and particles to a minimum by carefully choosing the items to be used onboard.

Every space shuttle is equipped with biocidal cleanser, disposable gloves, general-purpose wipes, and a vacuum cleaner. Astronauts wearing the gloves do a periodic cleanup with the cleanser and wipes in the waste-collection area and the galley and dining areas. They also use this

Carl Walz: Mission Specialist

Astronaut Carl Walz had the job of mission specialist-2 (MS-2) during space shuttle *Columbia* flight STS-65 in 1994. He found that the job had a lot of challenges. Basically, the MS-2 is the mission operations manager, or flight engineer. The MS-2 makes sure that the commander and pilot take care of everything on the flight checklist during both launch and landing. These key tasks must be performed flawlessly, or the entire success of the flight may be threatened and the lives of the entire crew may be put at risk. The MS-2 also tracks all equipment problems in a log book and takes on the responsibility for finding solutions to the problems. The MS-2 may also help the pilot and commander with switches on the cockpit panel located in front of his or her position on the flight deck.

Once the launch is complete, the shuttle shifts from rocket to space station, a sort of mobile outpost in the sky. The shuttle generally spends between five and eighteen days in space. During this time, items that won't be used until just before landing, such as space suits, bulky seats, and helmets, are stowed away. The MS-2 oversees this process and helps make sure the crew installs everything that is needed for a safe and effective journey. Cameras and photographic equipment are set up. Exercise equipment is installed in the most convenient place for each mission.

At the end of the mission, just before leaving orbit, the MS-2 makes sure the shuttle is ready to turn from "space station" to glider. In-flight equipment is exchanged for the space suits and seats used during launch. They will be needed again as the shuttle glides down through Earth's atmosphere to ensure a safe landing.

During missions that have astronauts working on double shifts, the MS-2 is often the commander of one of the shifts, while the commander and pilot sleep. Walz says this is both a great responsibility and a great honor. During the fifteen-day mission in 1994, he not only took care of all these key jobs, but he also carried out onboard experiments and photographed Earth. He says, "It is an experience I will remember for a long time."

Astronaut Carl E. Walz.

system for cleaning eating utensils and trays and mopping up anything that has spilled. Cabin walls and floors also get wiped down.

Housekeeping in space doesn't just mean cleaning house, though. It means taking care of anything that must be attended to on a regular basis but isn't part of the mission objectives. One of the most important systems that needs servicing is the Environmental Control and Life Support System. Does this sound important? It is. This system provides the shuttle interior with an atmosphere and climate that enables the crew to live in the harsh environment of space. One part of that system filters excess carbon dioxide out of the air. As the astronauts breathe, they naturally take in oxygen from the air and breathe out carbon dioxide. Living without filtration in a closed system such as the shuttle, the astronauts would soon find themselves breathing toxic levels of carbon dioxide. The air in the shuttle is passed through canisters of lithium hydroxide, which absorbs the carbon dioxide in the air. The air is then returned to the shuttle interior. These canisters have to be changed about once every twenty-four hours for a small crew of four, and about once every eleven hours for a large crew of seven.

Video and voice communications are exchanged with mission control in Houston, Texas, using a special antenna and a link to two communications relay satellites. However, mail also comes in over a thermal printer. One or two astronauts do the daily job of screening the messages and getting them to the right crew members in time for work schedules to be changed, if necessary.

The space shuttle is, without question, a busy place full of activity and daily chores. As one astronaut remarked, "I learn things on the shuttle just eating breakfast in the morning." Living onboard the shuttle in the weightlessness of space is a challenge in itself. And that's even without the payload jobs—the satellite that needs to be released, the EVA that needs to be done, the science laboratory experiments that need to be run, and the space station deliveries that need to be made. These tasks form the true heart of every mission.

This photo shows an astronaut during an extravehicular activity training at the Neutral Bouyancy Laboratory.

Chapter 5

Space Work

Ask any astronaut, and he or she will probably say the job is the greatest in the world. That's not to say it's easy, though! On every mission the unexpected can happen, and astronauts have to be ready to adapt quickly to a situation for which no one had planned. At the same time, every moment onboard the shuttle is valuable time. Even though the shuttle is reusable, every launch is costly. The opportunity to carry out a particular mission may occur infrequently—or only once. For example, positions of satellites change constantly, and a rendezvous may need to be timed precisely. So even though every astronaut has to be flexible to deal with the unexpected, every phase of a mission has to be prepared for and planned carefully and thoroughly.

On top of that, shuttle crews are operating in a very unusual environment—not at all like the one we live in every day. Therefore, training is a vital ingredient to a shuttle crew's success.

Training for Space

Since astronauts can't actually practice in space for tasks they plan to carry out in space, NASA has created machines or environments that try to mimic what the crews will experience while they are in orbit. One of the most important of these is the Neutral Buoyancy Laboratory, or buoyancy simulator, which is probably the largest indoor pool in the world. The idea is that people float in water much as they do in space. So this giant pool is just about the closest simulation we have on Earth of what it is like to float—and try to work—in space. The lab is really just a huge tank of water measuring 102 feet wide (31 m), 40 feet (12 m) deep, and 202 feet (62 m) long—about 40 feet (12 m) longer than an Olympic-size swimming pool. The pool is big enough to hold a full-size replica of the shuttle payload bay. It's also big enough to hold a full-size replica of the ISS. This is where astronauts train for space walks. Astronauts in training don't swim in this water (it won't help them maneuver in space). Instead, they try to move as they would in orbit. The training tools they use are designed to be as neutral in the water as possible—that is, they neither sink nor float. The astronauts practice the actual tasks they expect to perform during an EVA, and they even wear space suits (also known as Extravehicular Activity Mobility Units, or EMUs).

NASA also has two Shuttle Mission Simulators—one that pitches and yaws and rolls the way a shuttle might, and another that doesn't move. Astronauts get used to living in these environments while the commander and pilot concentrate on training at the consoles. Meanwhile, the training team can hear everything crew members say to each other and what switches they try to flip when a system "fails." This gives the training team a good idea of how much the astronauts know and how they'll react in case of emergencies.

The training team is important to every shuttle crew. It's up to this team to come up with simulated crises—the worst possibilities they can think of that might happen during a particular mission. The team throws these problems out to the crew. What would the crew do if several systems failed at once? How would it bring the shuttle home safely?

The Shuttle Engineering Simulator (SES) provides consoles just like the ones found at the rear of the flight deck. These are the manual controls the pilot and commander use when they are pulling the shuttle close to a satellite or spacecraft for a rendezvous in space. Controls just like the ones that work the robotic arm are also located here, and astronauts who will be working with this giant crane-like machine extension spend a lot of time training on the SES.

The Vertical Motion Simulator (VMS) provides the commander and pilot with a highly accurate simulation of the landing process. The crew can fly in simulation down to the final approach, landing, and final rollout of the shuttle. The VMS provides visual images that look especially real, which helps the crew get a good sense of what it's really like to land a shuttle.

The Shuttle Training Aircraft (STA) shows crews in training what it's like to fly during a different part of the landing—the steep dive that a shuttle takes just before landing. Most aircraft come toward the ground at about a 3-degree gliding approach—but not the shuttle. To land it correctly, the astronaut at the controls has to take it into a steep slope that resembles a "dive-bombing." This is necessary because the shuttle is so massive and doesn't glide very well. Practice with landing is very important. The commander cannot rev the engines and take the shuttle around for another approach, as an airplane pilot can. The shuttle doesn't have the engines or equipment to do that. So the commander has to get it right the first time. Using the STA (which does have engines to get the astronaut out of a tight spot), commanders and pilots make hundreds of approaches until they are sure they have a perfect feel for what the shuttle will do. Experienced commanders and pilots say the real thing feels almost exactly like the simulator they used for training.

Even photography gets practiced. Full-scale replicas of the orbiter (except for the wings) allow the crews to practice getting the perfect picture from the cabin or from the payload bay. They also practice getting ready for an EVA—getting familiar with the checklist and the equipment they'll need to use and learning the procedures they must follow perfectly. One forgotten step could cause an astronaut's death as he or she steps out into the unforgiving environment of space.

NASA even has an EMU Caution and Warning Simulator to train astronauts in the safe use of their space suits. The space suits, of course, have to have their own life-support systems. They also have communications systems and caution and warning systems. Crew members have to be completely at home with all of these systems and ready to respond to them quickly and calmly, so they train with the controls found on the EMU's display and control module. There's also an EVA Vacuum Chamber, which lets EVA crew members test their EMU suits and their preparations for EVAs. This experience helps crew members feel confident about their suits in the vacuum of space.

NASA has many more simulators and training programs, but this short list gives you an idea of how much training the crews go through. In addition, crews in training spend a lot of time in the gym working out. Their job is very physically demanding—especially space walks. Even though the astronauts are weightless in space, getting a job done often requires considerable exertion, strength, and flexibility. So keeping in shape is important for the astronauts.

Using the Robot Arm

The shuttle's robot arm is supplied by Canada, so it is known as Canadarm. It is also sometimes referred to as the Shuttle Remote Manipulator System (SRMS). (The Canadian space agency has also developed a more complex version of this tool for the ISS.) The first Canadarm flew on the very first shuttle flight, STS-1, aboard the space shuttle *Columbia*. This giant arm is fastened in the payload bay and is essential for almost all situations in which the shuttle mission calls for either deploying or retrieving an object to or from space. Most recently, it played key roles in the assembly of the ISS, beginning with the joining of the U.S. Unity node with Russia's Zarya control module.

From inside the shuttle cabin an astronaut moves the controls, which in turn move the arm. The arm is strong, yet it can handle delicate instruments with precision and gentleness. Moving it is something like controlling the steam shovel that picks up prizes in an arcade game. It takes careful, precise, controlled hand movements on the part of the crew member at the controls. But Canadarm does all the heavy lifting!

The Shuttle Remote Manipulator System, Canadarm, provides the muscle power as astronut Scott E. Parazynski moves a bulky piece of equipment. Canadarm2 can also be seen in the lower left corner of the photo.

Canadarm is made up of three joints—shoulder, elbow, and wrist—separated by two long booms that form the upper and lower arm. The whole instrument weighs 905 pounds (410 kg), but it can handle a load that would weigh 585,000 pounds (266,000 kg) on Earth.

Satellite Send-Off

A satellite deployment is among the most exciting moments onboard the shuttle, especially when the satellite will be doing exciting work. That was definitely the case when astronaut Cady Coleman directed the deployment of the *Chandra X-Ray Observatory*. (It is named after the late Indian-American astrophysicist Subrahmanyan Chandrasekhar,

This photo shows the *Chandra X-Ray Observatory* just before it was tilted upward and released from the space shuttle *Columbia*'s payload bay.

who was called Chandra by everyone who knew him.) Coleman was reading a book about the *X-ray* view of the universe, and she observed, "By the time I finish this book, they will have rewritten it," thanks to the way the *Chandra* telescope was about to open up a new understanding of the universe. It was especially built to detect *X-ray* emissions from faraway objects—objects no one had ever seen in this way before.

As the time for the *telescope* deployment came up on the crew's schedule, the astronauts opened the huge doors of the payload bay. Then they checked on the health of the telescope. This payload carried its own rocket because *Chandra* was scheduled to travel in an unusual orbit that would send it as far from Earth as one-third of the

station *Mir.* On that mission, Collins and commander James Wetherbee had to solve the problem of a leaky thruster before they could risk pulling close to *Mir.* They deftly pulled up within 37 feet (11 m) of the big Russian space station, then backed off to hover 400 feet (120 m) away.

Equipment problems also arose while Collins commanded *Columbia.* An electrical short caused a set of computers linked to the shuttle's main engines to fail. A display in the cockpit also went out. Because of an engine fuel leak, the shuttle could not fly to the orbit that was originally planned for it. In the cargo bay, *Columbia* was carrying a 50,162-pound (22,753-kg) astronomical instrument—the $1.5 billion *Advanced X-Ray Astrophysics Facility* (AXAF) imaging system, better known as the *Chandra X-Ray Observatory.* In spite of all the setbacks, Collins kept the mission right on schedule, and her crew released the satellite on time, in perfect working order. Using its own rocket, *Chandra* climbed to its planned orbit, extending as far as 86,458 miles (139,141 km) above Earth. From there it has sent back brilliant images and information about such mysterious objects as *black holes,* exploding stars, and *quasars.*

Collins says that, as a child, she admired pilots, astronauts, and explorers. She didn't know then that her dream of becoming one of them would come true. As she made her historic liftoff, guided her mission, and glided out of the skies and back to Earth, she hoped that young people—both male and female—would see her mission and reach for their own dreams. "Because," she adds, "dreams do come true!"

distance to the Moon, so the crew also checked to make sure the rocket had made the trip to orbit safely. Coleman began moving through her checklist. Each step was timed down to the minute, and the crew had trained for this moment carefully. If anything went wrong, they were prepared to exit the cabin into the airlessness of the cargo bay on an emergency EVA to do any needed repairs. Luckily, that wasn't necessary.

The big telescope was lifted into position, ready for release. The final okay was given by flight controllers in Houston, and at the Chandra Operations Control Center in Cambridge, Massachusetts. Everything looked good.

The electrical power cables that hooked *Chandra* into the shuttle's electrical system were disconnected. The telescope's internal battery power would keep it running until it could unfurl its solar panels and run off the power provided by the Sun. Then Coleman and mission specialist Michel Tognini ejected the big telescope from the payload bay. As *Chandra* moved out into space, commander Eileen Collins and pilot Jeff Ashby gently edged *Columbia* safely out of the way. *Chandra*'s rocket ignited and the heaviest payload ever carried by a shuttle was safely on its way.

Satellite Rescue Squad at Work

The story of the *Hubble Space Telescope* is one of the greatest of all satellite-repair success stories. Shuttle crews had repaired satellites before, lengthening the lives of important and expensive instruments. But the *Hubble* story had become a long and frustrating one.

Scientists had had to wait several years past schedule for the *Hubble Space Telescope* to be carried into orbit by a shuttle. The *Challenger* tragedy had set back all flight schedules. Finally, in April 1990, this exciting visible-light telescope was launched from the cargo bay of the space shuttle *Discovery*, STS-31. But the initial images sent to Earth from this technologically advanced telescope were disappointing. As it turned out, there was a flaw in the telescope's main mirror, which affected its ability to gather light and produce clear images. The flaw had escaped notice, and many scientists blamed cost-cutting for the oversight. The long-awaited *Hubble Space Telescope* was orbiting Earth, but it just couldn't see as well as everyone had expected it would. Its images were blurred and vague, even though it orbited high above Earth's atmosphere (which prevents very clear images from being taken).

The mistake was a major embarrassment to NASA, but not a disaster for *Hubble*. Teams of scientists and engineers came up with a solution—a corrective lens that could be installed on the telescope to make up for the flaw in the mirror. A repair mission was launched on December 2, 1993. It was up to the crew aboard the space shuttle *Endeavour*, STS-61, to make the repair. The crew had some difficulty locking onto the *Hubble*, but Swiss mission specialist Claude Nicollier grabbed it with the robot Canadarm and pulled it into the

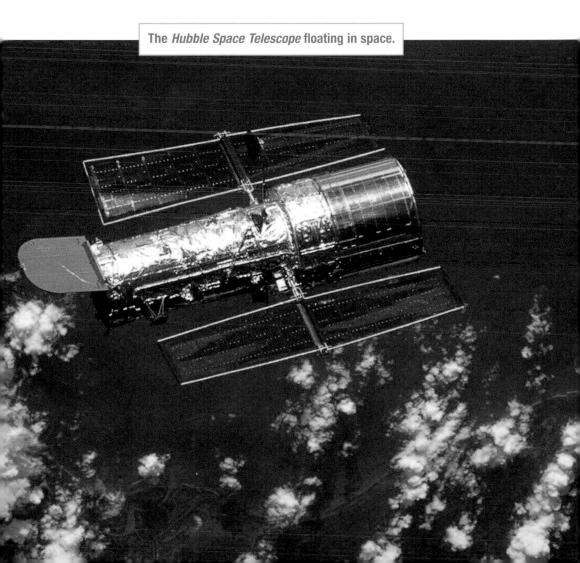

The *Hubble Space Telescope* floating in space.

shuttle's cargo bay, where it was carefully secured. Later that same day, December 4, shuttle crew members performed the first of a series of EVAs in the airless bay.

The ordeal of the crew members that day provides a good example of the kind of detail and hard work this kind of operation entails. The space walk that followed lasted seven hours and fifty minutes, the second-longest EVA in NASA history. Story Musgrave and Jeffrey Hoffman were the first astronauts to work on *Hubble*. The next day, Kathy Thornton and Tom Akers followed up with another EVA to replace damaged solar arrays on the telescope. Musgrave and Hoffman performed three more EVAs on the following days. All the astronauts had undergone extensive underwater training to prepare for the unusually tricky requirements of this project.

On the first day, Musgrave and Hoffman started early. They entered the cargo bay and unpacked their tools, safety tethers, and work platforms. They traveled to the required area of the telescope by using a foot restraint and platform attached to the end of the robot arm. Inside the shuttle, Nicollier controlled the arm, moving Hoffman around the telescope. At the same time, Musgrave worked to install protective coverings on key areas of the telescope to keep them from being damaged during the EVA. Then the astronauts opened the doors to the telescope's equipment bay and installed a foot restraint there to keep them from floating freely.

Everything went smoothly with the day's project—replacing two sets of the gyroscopes that keep the *Hubble* pointing in the right direction. The astronauts also did some other maintenance tasks and prepared for the next day's EVA. Then trouble hit. They could not rebolt the door to the gyroscope bay. The stubborn astronauts would not give

Everyone knows that when you throw a stone up in the air, it comes back down to Earth. So why don't satellites fall out of the sky? Well, they do if they aren't launched high enough, in the right direction, and with great enough velocity (or if they later lose speed for some reason).

As you'll recall, in the late seventeenth century Isaac Newton first offered a thorough description of the principles of motion and gravitation that make orbits work. (1) He said that when something is motionless, it tends to remain motionless (inertia); when something is moving, it tends to keep moving (momentum). (2) The degree of force exerted on an object and the mass of the object determine how much the object's position changes. (3) For every action there is an equal and opposite reaction (the same principle that makes rockets work).

So as a satellite is launched by a rocket speeding through space, the satellite moves in a straight line away from Earth. However, if it is not moving fast enough to get away from Earth's *gravitational field,* it is pulled toward Earth. If its speed is great enough, though, it will not fall back directly to Earth. It will continue to orbit.

The satellite's continuing momentum keeps it from falling and yet Earth's gravity keeps tugging. So the satellite is constantly "falling around Earth"—another way of saying that it is orbiting.

Isaac Newton.

up, though. With advice coming from engineers in Houston, who thought the change in temperature had made this task difficult, Musgrave and Hoffman worked at the top and the bottom of the doors at the same time. Finally, they closed.

By the end of the mission, though, all the maintenance and repairs were taken care of. The optical correction package was in place. The solar arrays were working like new. The new gyroscopes were in place. And the doors to the gyroscope bay had closed. The team had done its job, and the *Hubble Space Telescope* was ready to go back to work. Nicollier used Canadarm again to move the telescope out of the payload bay and away from the shuttle. Gentle firings of *Endeavour's* small maneuvering jets carefully moved the shuttle away from the telescope.

The repair was a huge success. *Hubble* has gone on to take beautiful, clear images. It has discovered that there are some 50 billion more galaxies in the universe than was previously believed. It has captured stunning pictures of galaxies, stars, and the planets in our own solar system. Additional repair missions by shuttle crews have extended the telescope's life many years beyond the original plans. The *Hubble Space Telescope* is truly a space-shuttle success story.

Scientists in Microgravity

Before the beginning of the space age, we were able to observe only natural processes as they occur on Earth—under the pull of Earth's gravity. It was next to impossible to figure out how gravity affects everyday natural processes such as plant growth, blood circulation, crystal growth, or even a clock ticking. The space shuttle gives us a unique laboratory to study these processes in microgravity—almost completely without the effect of Earth's gravity. This possibility helps scientists understand the processes better. It also helps us figure out how the processes might work on other planets and moons. It is absolutely necessary for planning future long-term missions such as piloted voyages to Mars and the Moon.

STS-58 *Columbia* (October 18 to November 1, 1993) was a fourteen-day research mission dedicated to life-science research aboard Spacelab. During this record-length shuttle mission, the crew conducted neurovestibular, cardiovascular, cardiopulmonary, metabolic, and musculoskeletal research. The scientists onboard the shuttle made use of the microgravity of space to reveal fundamentals of physiology that Earth's gravity normally makes it difficult to detect.

More recently, on the same mission that carried the *Chandra X Ray Observatory* into space, crew members performed thirteen experiments in the shuttle cabin. They ranged from an amateur radio experiment to cell-culture tests. They also included calibrating *ultraviolet-*, infrared-, and visible-radiation sensors on a satellite. Crew members investigated plant growth in microgravity. They used video to record the changes and responses in the plants. They also evaluated the effect of launch, microgravity, and reentry conditions on a set of microelectrical mechanical devices. Coordinating the complex steps required to carry out experiments like these requires careful attention to detail, accuracy, and efficiency. As Cady Coleman says, it means you have to be able to work well at top speed—a challenge she says she likes.

Without question, work onboard a space shuttle is never dull.

Russia's *Mir* space station.

Chapter 6

Ambassadors in Space

While NASA had been thinking about building a space station for a long time, Russian cosmonauts actually had been launching and operating space stations for years. In 1971, which was early in the history of space exploration, the Soviet space program began launching space stations in which cosmonauts lived in space for several months at a time and carried out scientific research. Starting with a small habitat, they used powerful rockets to launch these space stations in large sections, or modules. The first mission to the small habitat, *Salyut 1,* arrived aboard the spacecraft *Soyuz 10.* The crew members docked but did not succeed in boarding the space station, so they returned home. The second crew arrived aboard *Soyuz 11* and spent just over three weeks at the *Salyut 1* space station, from June 7 to 29, 1971, in what promised to be the first successful space station mission. This mission set a record, but the voyage home ended in tragedy. A pressure equalization valve got stuck open when *Soyuz 11* detached from the space station. The spacecraft cabin lost oxygen and pressure. The three crew members were not wearing pressure suits and all of them died.

The Soviets pressed on, but after that point, all cosmonauts were required to wear pressure suits during launch, reentry, and docking. The USSR launched a second space station, *Salyut 2,* in 1973, but it failed to stay in orbit. From 1974 on, though, the Soviets launched and maintained at least one space station in orbit almost continuously for the rest of the twentieth century. They continued to focus on gaining experience and knowledge about long-duration human spaceflight. The last and best of the *Salyut* series, *Salyut 7,* was launched in 1982 and remained in orbit until 1991. Finally, their greatest space station, *Mir,* arrived in orbit in 1986 and remained there until March 28, 2001, when it reentered Earth's atmosphere over the Pacific Ocean.

Meanwhile, NASA had not developed a space station as part of its program to reach the Moon. Instead, the agency had used massive rocket power to lift spacecraft directly from Earth's surface and escape Earth's orbit to travel to the Moon. But once the United States reached the Moon, a lot of the congressional funding and public support for the U.S. space program evaporated. The United States was deeply involved in a costly war in Vietnam, and the Moon race had already been "won."

For the United States the delay in the development of the space shuttle meant that ideas about a space station had to go on hold. However, NASA engineers did put together an ingenious space station called *Skylab* in the early 1970s. It was pieced together from spare parts left over from the Apollo program and became the home and scientific laboratory of three crews of three astronauts in 1973 and 1974. NASA had intended to send other crews to *Skylab* aboard the space shuttle. However, the shuttle program developed too slowly. By 1979 *Skylab* could not maintain its orbit without a nudge of power. NASA had no way to provide it with the needed power, and the first shuttle flight was still two years away. So the only U.S. space station ever built ended in a fiery plunge through Earth's atmosphere.

A New Space Habitat

Finally, in the 1980s, the United States and several other countries began work on the International Space Station (ISS). Funding for this project was not easy for NASA to obtain. Some people worried that other countries might be unable to keep their commitments for providing important parts of the structure. If that happened, the United States could not afford to complete the space station alone; the project was too vast, and the money already spent would be lost. The U.S. Congress debated the pros and cons of funding the project. And as NASA's funding faltered, all the partner countries worried that *they* would be the ones to lose money.

For anyone interested in the human exploration of space, the concept of an international space station was attractive. A space station could provide a foothold in space as a starting point for crews on their way to the Moon or Mars. At the same time it would provide a permanent space laboratory—a place to study the nature of substances and the effects of weightlessness on them. Manufacturing in space might also become possible—an idea that is especially useful to manufacturers of high-precision computer chips, polymers, crystals, and other products that can be formed perfectly without the distortions caused by gravity.

Space Station Life: Learning on Mir

The Soviet space stations were designed to provide a place where astronauts could live for long periods of time. They were built to explore the human endurance challenges posed by long-duration missions in space and to study the effects of living and working in space.

The last of the Soviet space stations, *Mir* (meaning "Peace" or "World"), welcomed its first crew in February 1986. This new space station could house scientific experiments and long-term crews—usually three cosmonauts at a time. A shuttle craft called *Soyuz* could be launched with supplies and trade-off crews, but one member of the crew usually remained onboard for an extended stay, often up to a year or more. *Mir* succeeded in establishing a virtually permanent human presence in space.

In 1989 an enormous shift in the political scene changed the exploration of space. The Communist government of the Soviet Union, which had been hostile toward the United States for decades, lost its power and dissolved. The USSR broke into separate countries, the largest of which is Russia. These political changes led to an enormous new opportunity for the space agencies of the two former rivals to work together. A new era of cooperation began and new possibilities were explored. NASA established a program to set the groundwork for exchanging knowledge with the Russian space agency—a luxury that had been possible only on unofficial levels in the past. Russian cosmonauts flew in the space shuttle. American astronauts flew on *Mir*. International cooperation was sought in building a space station. Now Russia could make use of NASA's shuttle, while NASA could begin to learn from Russian cosmonauts' experience with living in space for extended periods.

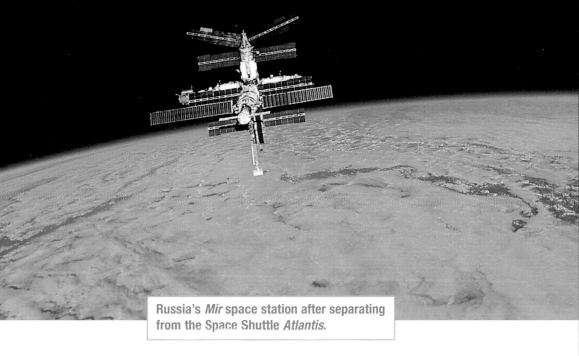

Russia's *Mir* space station after separating
from the Space Shuttle *Atlantis*.

The United States and Russia could also test whether the two
nations could work together. Could a docking hatch be made so that
the shuttle could dock with *Mir*? Could the shuttle be maneuvered to
rendezvous and dock at a space station? Could astronauts and cosmonauts live and work together? Could American ground crews manage
to function in a way that fit patterns and traditions that the Russian
teams already had in place? The first phase of the program consisted of
eleven space shuttle flights involving *Mir* from December 1994 to
June 1998. During that time, seven U.S. astronauts joined Russian
cosmonauts onboard *Mir* one by one. It was a brilliant plan, using

Shuttle Missions to *Mir*

Vital Statistics

Shuttle Mission	Launch Date	Mission at *Mir*
STS-60	2/3/1994	Crew includes Russian cosmonaut Sergei Krikalev, making this the first joint U.S.-Russian spaceflight since the Apollo-Soyuz mission in 1975—a step toward cooperation for the future shuttle missions to *Mir*.
STS-63	2/3/1995	First shuttle-*Mir* rendezvous; crew includes Russian cosmonaut Vladimir Titov.
STS-71	6/27/1995	First shuttle-*Mir* docking; mission carries two cosmonauts to *Mir* and picks up U.S. astronaut Norm Thagard and two cosmonauts, who arrived at *Mir* aboard a Russian Soyuz spacecraft in March 1995.
STS-74	11/12/1995	Delivers docking module for use on all remaining shuttle-*Mir* flights; astronauts from the European Space Agency (ESA), Canada, the United States, and Russia work together in space for the first time.
STS-76	3/22/1996	Carries U.S. astronaut Shannon Lucid to *Mir*; U.S. astronauts perform first American space walk on a Russian spacecraft.
STS-79	9/16/1996	Carries U.S. astronaut John Blaha to *Mir* and picks up Shannon Lucid at the end of her six-month tour.
STS-81	1/12/1997	Picks up John Blaha and leaves astronaut Jerry Linenger; delivers a record amount of supplies and experiments.

Shuttle Mission	Launch Date	Mission at *Mir*
STS-84	5/15/1997	Picks up Jerry Linenger and leaves astronaut Michael Foale; Russian cosmonaut Elena Kondakova and ESA astronaut Jean-François Clervoy are also on the crew.
STS-86	9/25/1997	Picks up Michael Foale and leaves astronaut Dave Wolf; Vladimir Titov becomes first cosmonaut to perform a shuttle-based EVA.
STS-89	1/22/1998	Picks up Dave Wolf and leave astronaut Andy Thomas.
STS-91	6/2/1998	Ninth and final shuttle-*Mir* docking: NASA astronaut Andy Thomas heads home.

existing U.S. shuttle orbiters and the Russian space station to build joint space experience and begin scientific research that the two nations could continue together.

One veteran U.S. astronaut, Shannon Lucid, spent 188 days onboard with Russian cosmonauts Yuri Onufrienko and Yuri Usachev. Her mission lasted from March 22 through September 26, 1996. By the end of her stay, she had logged more hours in orbit than any other woman in the world and the most flight hours in orbit of any non-Russian.

Trouble Onboard

Generally, the Russian and American crew members found they had a lot in common. They often felt they were healing wounds as ambassadors from their respective countries. One group looked back over the previous twenty years and realized that not long before they had been poised, ready for battle, on opposite sides of the Cold War's "Iron Curtain"—a symbol that we might think of today as a virtual wall of differing ideas and objectives. Although no "curtain" existed, the political division was very real.

Not all went smoothly for the cosmonauts and astronauts, though. Originally designed to serve a three-year mission span, the *Mir* space station had now been in orbit for a dozen years. Since the change in government, Russia was less prosperous than before, and no money was available for repairs and replacements. Equipment began to wear out and things began to go wrong. A fire broke out onboard during one astronaut's stay. A robot delivery spacecraft collided with the station during another mission, leaving the station damaged.

Andy Thomas was the last U.S. astronaut to visit the big, rundown space station. He arrived in January 1998 and the shuttle returned to pick him up almost six months later. He returned home onboard STS-91 on June 12, 1998.

Finally, on March 22, 2001, the 143-ton space station ended its long and useful career. Under control by Russian space agency ground crews, *Mir* plunged into the Pacific Ocean in a blaze of fire. For more than fifteen years it had tirelessly orbited Earth. It was home to countless significant scientific experiments. Cosmonauts living and working onboard *Mir* had set many endurance records—some lasting more than a year. *Mir* was built bit by bit over its life span, and it hosted the most extensive continuous human presence ever maintained in space.

Chapter 7

Space Station for a Planet

The Russian and American crew members cooperated well aboard *Mir* and on space shuttle flights. Yet the governments of the two countries often still had trouble ironing out difficulties and establishing trust. This extended to their space agencies. Conflicts surrounding the schedule and construction of the ISS developed while progress on its construction slowed.

Eventually, though, progress was made. It began at an opportune time, as *Mir*'s orbit deteriorated and the sprawling space station plunged to its fiery end. The ISS could now replace *Mir* as a permanent habitat in space. It would soon become a new island in orbit, a place where scientific work and manufacturing could take place.

Ultimately, it might even serve as a depot, or way station, for more distant voyages to the Moon or perhaps to Mars.

Experiences on *Mir* provided engineers with many insights for the design of the ISS. This huge joint project has involved many more nations than just the United States and Russia, including Canada, Japan, and the European Space Agency. No engineering project of this size and complexity has ever been attempted before, and the coordination of participating countries and private companies has been and continues to be a very difficult task.

The first ISS pieces were ready to haul to space in late 1998. The central piece, the Russian control module Zarya, was the first to arrive, launched from Star City in Kazakhstan, near Moscow. The second piece, called the Unity Node, was provided by the United States and was carried to the ISS by the space shuttle *Endeavour* in December 1998. The shuttle crew attached the two modules, activated the Zarya control module, and set up communications equipment during three EVAs. Unity serves as a passageway to Zarya and as a docking port for additional modules—including the U.S. Laboratory, the U.S. Habitation module, and an air lock.

Over the following months, five out of eight shuttle flights were devoted primarily to space-station assembly. In July 2000, a Russian Proton rocket launched the Zvezda module—the other primary Russian hardware contribution. This module provided support systems for all the early modules and living quarters for the first crews to arrive. By early November the first crew had arrived aboard a Russian Soyuz spacecraft. This spacecraft stayed at the station to provide an emergency escape vehicle for the crews.

At the end of November, *Endeavour* carried key communications and power source equipment to the station, including U.S. solar power arrays. By February 2001, the space shuttle *Atlantis*, STS-98, had arrived with the U.S. laboratory module known as Destiny. The ISS was growing rapidly.

Moving Vans for Space

The space shuttle orbiters had become giant moving vans. On the ground the huge doors of the shuttle payload bays swung open for packing. This was no simple packing job, though. Many decisions had to be made about the order in which items would be needed. Some materials—such as food and water for space-station crews could not be exposed to the extreme temperatures and the vacuum of space. Yet they would have to ride in the uninsulated payload bay. The management of the details of an operation like this is known as *logistics,* and logistical questions like these received a lot of thought before the first launch to build the ISS ever took place.

Pressurized modules, or containers, were designed to fit neatly into the shuttle bay. One type, designed by the Italian Space Agency, is called the Multi-Purpose Logistics module (MPLM). It is designed to travel onboard the shuttle to transport laboratory racks filled with equipment, experiments, and supplies to and from the ISS. The first of these was flown to the space station aboard STS-102 in March 2001. It remained mounted inside the payload bay until after the shuttle docked with the space station. Once the shuttle docked, the crew used the shuttle's robot Canadarm to move the MPLM from the payload bay to the Unity module, where it was docked at one of Unity's six hatches.

The Russian-built Zarya (left) and U.S. built Unity modules were photographed shortly after Unity left *Endeavor*'s cargo bay.

While the MPLM is docked, its cargo of racks and components are transferred to the space station. Once the crew has finished unloading this big "moving van," it can load unneeded equipment and trash from the space station for the trip back to Earth. Then the MPLM is undocked and returned to the shuttle bay.

Similar concepts are used by a company called SPACEHAB, which has designed many different modules that stow materials and equipment in lockers and special racks.

Susan Helms is one of the three people who made up the second crew to live and work aboard the ISS. The crew arrived at the ISS aboard STS-102 *Discovery* on March 9, 2001, for a stay that would last for six to eight months. Helms first began flying aboard jets as a career engineer in the U.S. Air Force. Before long she found herself hooked on flying. Poor eyesight kept her from becoming a pilot like her father had been, but that didn't stop her. As a flight-test engineer, Helms had flown in thirty different types of U.S. and Canadian military aircraft.

Soon she began wondering, "How can I fly higher and faster than I am right now?" She began to realize that space was the answer. What next? "I just put my application in, of course, never expecting to get selected," she explains modestly.

As the daughter of a career Air Force pilot, Helms thinks her interest in the Air Force was ingrained from birth. Helms also enjoys jogging, reading, computers, and music. In fact, the talented space-station engineer plays keyboard for MAX-Q, a rock-and-roll band.

Astronaut Susan J. Helms.

Shuttle Service Begins

The first expedition crew to arrive at the ISS was launched by Russia aboard a Soyuz spacecraft on October 31, 2000. So the first "shuttle service" for crew members of the ISS began at the end of the first crew's mission. They returned to Earth aboard the space shuttle *Discovery*, STS-102, in March 2001. They exchanged places with the members of the second crew, who traveled to the station aboard the shuttle.

Today the ISS is still a baby compared to *Mir*, but it is growing rapidly. The space shuttle has provided most of the transportation for carrying the ISS modules to space piece by piece. Once they are there, astronauts and cosmonauts join them together. The space shuttle crews have played a key part in learning how to build in space, beginning the construction, transportation, and installation of new modules and providing service, maintenance, and other "freighter" duties to the big "Tinkertoy in space."

The space shuttle has begun doing its original job at last, and is doing it well. In the process, major strides have been made in international cooperation and coordination. Astronauts have learned to speak Russian. Cosmonauts have learned to speak English. Both have learned a lot about each other's cultures. Meanwhile, Italian, Canadian, French, and Japanese astronauts and others have flown and worked onboard the space shuttle. A new era has dawned—one in which the countries of the world work together. As nations learn to understand one another better through working together toward the same goals, perhaps another, greater benefit may be gained. Perhaps Lyndon B. Johnson was right when he said in 1958, "Men [and women] who have worked together to reach the stars are not likely to descend together to the depths of war."

Vital Statistics

Name of Orbiter and Flight Number	Date Launched	Selected Mission Facts
COLUMBIA, STS-1	4/12/1981	First flight to space
CHALLENGER, STS-7	6/18/1983	Sally K. Ride is first woman U.S. astronaut
COLUMBIA, STS-9	11/28/1983	First mission to carry six people into space at once; first flight, ESA-NASA Spacelab-1
CHALLENGER, STS-41C	4/6/1984	*Long Duration Exposure Facility* (LDEF)
CHALLENGER, STS-51L	1/28/1986	Accidental explosion destroys shuttle orbiter and crew
DISCOVERY, STS-26	9/29/1988	Space shuttle's return to space
ATLANTIS, STS-30	5/4/1989	*Magellan* (spacecraft mission to Venus) launched
ATLANTIS, STS-34	10/18/1989	*Galileo* (spacecraft mission to Jupiter and its four largest moons) launched
DISCOVERY, STS-31	4/24/1990	*Hubble Space Telescope* launched
DISCOVERY, STS-41	10/6/1990	*Ulysses* (spacecraft mission to the Sun) launched
ATLANTIS, STS-37	4/5/1991	*Compton Gamma Ray Observatory* launched

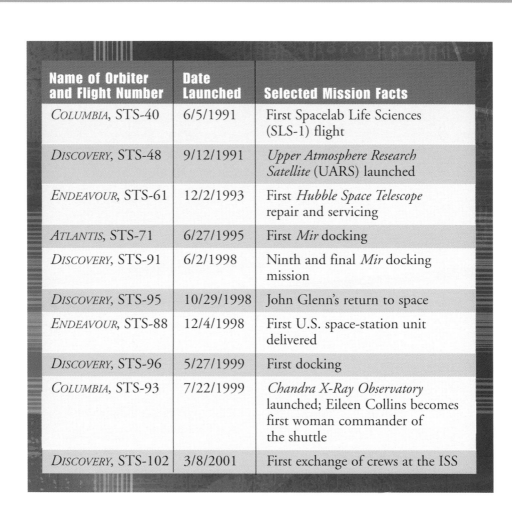

Name of Orbiter and Flight Number	Date Launched	Selected Mission Facts
COLUMBIA, STS-40	6/5/1991	First Spacelab Life Sciences (SLS-1) flight
DISCOVERY, STS-48	9/12/1991	*Upper Atmosphere Research Satellite* (UARS) launched
ENDEAVOUR, STS-61	12/2/1993	First *Hubble Space Telescope* repair and servicing
ATLANTIS, STS-71	6/27/1995	First *Mir* docking
DISCOVERY, STS-91	6/2/1998	Ninth and final *Mir* docking mission
DISCOVERY, STS-95	10/29/1998	John Glenn's return to space
ENDEAVOUR, STS-88	12/4/1998	First U.S. space-station unit delivered
DISCOVERY, STS-96	5/27/1999	First docking
COLUMBIA, STS-93	7/22/1999	*Chandra X-Ray Observatory* launched; Eileen Collins becomes first woman commander of the shuttle
DISCOVERY, STS-102	3/8/2001	First exchange of crews at the ISS

The Space Shuttle: A Timeline

1957 — The USSR puts the first artificial satellite, *Sputnik I*, into Earth orbit. A month later, *Sputnik II* is launched with a dog, Laika, onboard.

1958 — The United States successfully launches an artificial satellite, *Explorer 1*, into Earth orbit.

1961 — Yuri Gagarin becomes the first human in space.

Alan Shepard becomes the first American astronaut to enter space, piloting the Mercury spacecraft *Freedom 7*.

1962 — John Glenn orbits Earth in the Mercury spacecraft *Friendship 7*.

1969 — *Apollo 11* astronauts Neil Armstrong and Buzz Aldrin are the first humans to land on the Moon.

1972 — The space shuttle program is officially authorized.

1977–78 — The space shuttle *Enterprise* makes five test flights, taking off piggyback on a Boeing 747 and landing on its own at Edwards Air Force Base, California.

1981 — The first spaceflight of the Space Transportation System (STS) is made by the space shuttle *Columbia,* piloted by astronauts John W. Young and Robert L. Crippen.

1982 — On the fifth shuttle flight, two communications satellites become the first satellites deployed from a space shuttle.

1983 — On the seventh shuttle flight, aboard the space shuttle *Challenger,* Sally K. Ride becomes the first American woman in space.

The ninth shuttle flight, aboard *Columbia,* carries Spacelab in the cargo bay for the first time.

1986 — The twenty-fifth shuttle flight ends in an explosion less than two minutes after liftoff; all members of the *Challenger* crew die in the disaster. An investigation begins and flights are suspended for more than a year.

1988 — The space shuttle returns to space with the twenty-sixth mission, aboard *Discovery.*

1989 — Two planetary spacecraft are released from separate space shuttle flights: *Magellan,* a mission to Venus, and *Galileo,* a mission to Jupiter.

1990 — *Hubble Space Telescope,* the first of NASA's Great Observatories, is launched from the space shuttle *Discovery.*

1991 — The *Compton Gamma Ray Observatory* is launched from the space shuttle *Atlantis*; shuttle crew performs the first EVAs in five years.

1993 — During EVAs, space shuttle *Endeavour* astronauts install a corrective optical package (COSTAR) and perform other updates and repairs on the orbiting *Hubble Space Telescope.*

1997 — Space shuttle *Discovery* astronauts make five EVAs to update instruments aboard the *Hubble Space Telescope* in the second of three servicing missions.

1999 — *Chandra X-Ray Observatory,* another part of NASA's Great Observatories series, is launched and deployed from the space shuttle *Columbia.*

Third servicing mission for the *Hubble Space Telescope*: During three EVAs, astronauts onboard space shuttle *Discovery* perform maintenance on *HST,* possibly extending the telescope's mission another ten years.

First International Space Station docking by space shuttle *Discovery.* A second flight installs the first U.S. piece of the space station, a hub called the Unity Node.

2000 — A series of four shuttle flights focuses on transportation of ISS parts to orbit and installation at the space station.

2001 — First space shuttle transportation for an international space-station crew (second expedition crew).

Atlantis tries out a new, improved main engine, used for the first time.

Glossary

atmosphere—layers of gases surrounding Earth, forming the air we breathe; also gases surrounding another planet or moon

aurora (pl. aurorae)—a display of light caused by the interaction between energetic, charged particles and a planet's magnetic field

black hole—the collapsed core of a massive star that has reached the last stage of its life. The core is so small and dense that even light cannot travel fast enough to escape the star's powerful gravitational field.

booster—a rocket that adds a boost, or additional push, to the thrust of a main rocket or engine

cosmonaut—an astronaut in the Soviet or Russian space program

density—how much of a substance exists in a given volume of space

electromagnetic spectrum—the full range of the waves and frequencies of electromagnetic radiation. Radio waves and infrared rays, at one end of the spectrum, have very long wavelengths. Visible light is about in the middle. At the other end of the spectrum are types of radiation with such short wavelengths that they are invisible to humans, including ultraviolet (UV) waves, X rays, and gamma rays.

ergometer—an instrument that measures the amount of work performed by a muscle or a muscle group

escape velocity—the minimum velocity needed to escape the gravitational pull of a planet, such as Earth, or another body in space, such as the Moon. For Earth, escape velocity is roughly 25,010 miles per hour (11.18 km per second).

EVA—the acronym for extravehicular activity, which is a space walk

g-force—also known as a "g," a unit of force equal to the force of Earth's gravity on a body at rest at the surface

gravitational field—the region around an object in which its gravitational pull is felt

gravity—the force that pulls things toward the surface of a large object in space, such as a planet or moon; the attraction exerted by an object with mass

hypersonic—exceeding five times the speed of sound

logistics—the management of the details of an operation, especially seeing that needed supplies and personnel are in the right place at the right time

microgravity—in space, a condition where bodies are weightless and gravity is present only to an extremely small extent

NASA—the acronym for the National Aeronautics and Space Administration which is a U.S. space agency

orbit—the path traced by an object as it revolves around another body

oxidizer—a material that supplies oxygen so that combustion can take place in a rocket engine

power-gliding flight—in an aircraft, a flight using engine power to control descent and landing

quasar—a very bright object thought to be a young, energetic, and distant galaxy that is rapidly moving away from the Milky Way

recoil—the backward push of a gun when it is fired (an example of Newton's law that for every action there is an equal and opposite reaction)

revolve—to move in a path, or orbit, around another object. The Earth revolves around the Sun, making a complete trip in one year.

rocket thruster—a rocket used to change direction or boost speed

rotate—to turn on its axis. Earth rotates once a day.

surface tension—the force of attraction between water molecules

telescope—an instrument used to view distant objects, especially in space. Some telescopes observe in different regions of the electromagnetic spectrum, not just the visible-light region.

ultraviolet (UV) rays—radiation with wavelengths just shorter than violet light. "Black light" is a form of UV radiation.

velocity—the speed of an object in a named direction; different from speed, for which direction is not specified

X rays—radiation with wavelengths shorter than UV radiation but longer than gamma radiation

To Find Out More

The news from space changes fast, so it's always a good idea to check the copyright date on books, CD-ROMs, and videotapes to make sure that you are getting up-to-date information. One good place to look for current information from NASA is U.S. government depository libraries. There are several in each state.

Books

Campbell, Ann Jeanette. *The New York Public Library Amazing Space: A Book of Answers for Kids.* New York: John Wiley & Sons, 1997.

Caprara, Giovanni. *Living in Space: From Science Fiction to the International Space Station.* Willowdale, Ontario: Firefly Books, 2000.

Dyson, Marianne J. *Space Station Science: Life in Free Fall.* Illustrated by Dave Klug. With a foreword by Buzz Aldrin. New York: Scholastic, 1999.

Kettelkamp, Larry. *Living in Space.* New York: Morrow Junior Books, 1993.

Scott, Elaine. *Adventure in Space: The Flight to Fix the Hubble.* Photographs by Margaret Miller. New York: Hyperion Books for Children, 1995.

Spangenburg, Ray, and Kit Moser. *The Hubble Space Telescope.* Out of This World series. Danbury, Conn.: Grolier, Inc., 2002.

World Spaceflight News. *Challenger Accident: The Tragedy of Space Shuttle Flight 51-L and Its Aftermath.* Progressive Management, 2000.

Organizations and Online Sites

These organizations and sites are good sources of information about the space shuttle and spaceflight. Many of the sites listed are NASA sites that have links to many other interesting sources of information about the solar system. You can also sign up to receive NASA news on many subjects via e-mail.

Astronomical Society of the Pacific
http://www.aspsky.org
390 Ashton Avenue
San Francisco, CA 94112

The Astronomy Café
http://www2.ari.net/home/odenwald/cafe.html
This site answers questions and offers news and articles relating to astronomy and space. It is maintained by astronomer and NASA scientist Sten Odenwald.

NASA Ask a Space Scientist

http://image.gsfc.nasa.gov/poetry/ask/askmag.html#list

Take a look at the Interactive Page, where NASA scientists answer your questions about astronomy, space, and space missions. The site also has access to archives and fact sheets.

NASA History

http://history.nasa.gov

This in-depth site has information about all aspects of NASA history.

NASA Human Spaceflight

http://spaceflight.nasa.gov/index-m.html

This is the Internet hub for exploring everything related to human spaceflight, including stories and real-time data as they break. You can track space shuttle flights, explore the International Space Station, trace space history, and see many interesting images.

NASA Newsroom

http://www.nasa.gov/newsinfo/newsroom.html

This site features NASA's latest press releases, status reports, and fact sheets. It includes a news archive with past reports and a search button for the NASA website. You can even sign up for e-mail versions of all NASA press releases.

The Nine Planets: A Multimedia Tour of the Solar System

http://www.seds.org/nineplanets/nineplanets/nineplanets.html

This site has excellent material on the planets. It was created and is maintained by the Students for the Exploration and Development of Space at the University of Arizona.

Planetary Missions

http://nssdc.gsfc.nasa.gov/planetary/projects.html

At this site, you'll find NASA links to all current and past missions. It's a one-stop shopping center for a wealth of information.

The Planetary Society

http://www.planetary.org

65 North Catalina Avenue
Pasadena, CA 91106-2301

Real-Time Spacecraft Tracking

http://liftoff.msfc.nasa.gov/RealTime/JTrack/Spacecraft.html

Find out where the space shuttle (when in flight), ISS, *Hubble Space Telescope*, *Chandra X-Ray Observatory*, and other spacecraft are orbiting.

Sky Online

http://www.skypub.com

This is the website for *Sky and Telescope* magazine and other publications of Sky Publishing Corporation. You'll find a good weekly news section on general space and astronomy news. The site also has tips for amateur astronomers as well as a nice selection of links. A list of

science museums, planetariums, and astronomy clubs organized by state can help you locate nearby places to visit.

Welcome to the Planets

http://pds.jpl.nasa.gov/planets

This tour of the solar system has lots of pictures and information. The site was created and is maintained by the California Institute of Technology for NASA/Jet Propulsion Laboratory.

Windows to the Universe

http://windows.ivv.nasa.gov

This NASA site, developed by the University of Michigan, includes sections on "Our Planet," "Our Solar System," "Space Missions," and "Kids' Space." Choose from beginner, intermediate, or advanced presentation levels.

Places to Visit

Check the Internet (*www.skypub.com* is a good place to start), your local visitor's center, or your phone directory for planetariums and science museums near you. Here are a few suggestions.

Ames Research Center

Moffett Field, CA 94035

http://www.arc.nasa.gov

Located near Mountain View and Sunnyvale on the San Francisco Peninsula, Ames Research Center welcomes drop-in visitors. Admission is free.

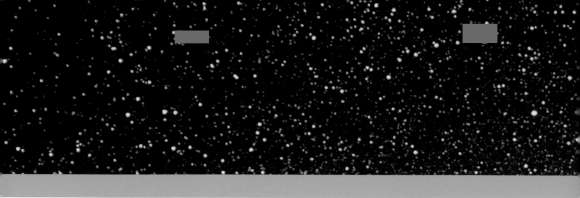

Exploratorium
3601 Lyon Street
San Francisco, CA 94123
http://www.exploratorium.edu
You'll find internationally acclaimed interactive science exhibits, including some on astronomy subjects.

National Air and Space Museum
7th and Independence Avenues., S.W.
Washington, DC 20560
http://www.nasm.edu/NASMDOCS/VISIT
This museum, located on the National Mall just west of the Capitol building, has all kinds of interesting exhibits.

Space Center Houston
Space Center Houston Information
1601 NASA Road 1
Houston, TX 77058
http://www.spacecenter.org
Space Center Houston offers a tour and exhibits related to humans in space, including a full-size space shuttle mock-up that lets you see inside the flight deck and mid-deck of the orbiter, from control consoles to sleeping quarters.

Spaceport USA
Kennedy Space Center
Titusville, FL 32899
http://www.kennedyspacecenter.com
This site offers a museum and special exhibits on the history of space exploration. The site includes a full-scale replica of the space shuttle *Explorer.*

U.S. Space and Rocket Center
P.O. Box 070015
Huntsville, AL 35807-7015
http://www.spacecamp.com/museum
This site offers exhibits of meteorites and rockets, Spacedome IMAX Theater, a full-scale mock-up of the Russian *Mir* space station, a full stack shuttle that includes the external fuel tank and boosters, and the homepage of the U.S. Space Camp, where participants learn about space exploration and space science by doing.

Bold numbers indicate illustrations.

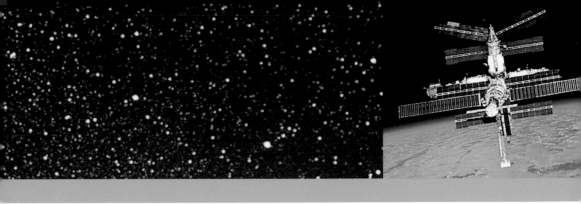

Ray Spangenburg and **Kit Moser** are a husband-and-wife writing team specializing in science and technology. They have written forty-five books and more than one hundred articles, including a five-book series on the history of science and a four-book series on the history of space exploration. As journalists, they covered NASA and related science activities for many years. They have flown on NASA's Kuiper Airborne Observatory, covered stories at the Deep Space Network in the Mojave Desert, and experienced zero gravity on experimental NASA flights out of NASA Ames Research Center. They live in Carmichael, California, with their Boston terrier, F. Scott Fitz.

Pluto

Uranus

Jupiter

Mars

Mercury

Sun